STEPPING UP

A Christian Approach to Stepparenting

Sean Alexander, Ph.D.

professional before attempting any techniques outlined in this book.

By reading this document, the reader agrees that the author or publisher is under no circumstances responsible for any losses, direct or indirect, incurred because of the use of the information contained within this document, including but not limited to errors, omissions, or inaccuracies.

CONTENTS

INTRODUCTION

The Calling of Christian Stepparents

Here's a reworded and paraphrased version:

Your path is unpredictable, with surprising developments and obstacles that can be intensely frustrating. Yet, it also brings instances of profound happiness. As a stepparent of faith, your role carries special significance. While managing daily challenges is essential, your mission extends beyond mere survival. No, you're called to create a thriving, Christ-centered blended family.

Now, I know what you're thinking. "Easier said than done!" And you're right. But hang in there because we're going to walk through this together. We'll explore the challenges, celebrate the victories, and discover how to bring God's love into every nook and cranny of your blended family life.

Let me introduce you to Sarah and Mike. Their story sounds familiar to you. Sarah was a single mom with two energetic boys, Jake (8) and Ethan (6), when she bumped into Mike at a church potluck. Mike, a widower with a 10-year-old daughter named Lily, was immediately smitten by Sarah's warm smile and infectious laugh. As they bonded over shared casseroles and Bible study discussions, they realized God might be writing a new chapter in their lives.

Their whirlwind romance led to a proposal six months later, with Sarah tearfully saying yes. But as the wedding day approached, both felt excitement and a healthy dose of panic. How on earth were they going to blend their families? Would the kids accept their new stepparent? And most importantly, how could they honor God in this new family dynamic?

If you're nodding along, thinking, "Yep, that sounds about right," you're not alone. The first few months after the wedding were a rollercoaster. Jake and Ethan tested Mike's daily patience with mischief and occasional sass. Lily, still grieving the loss of her mom, gave Sarah the cold shoulder and sometimes outright hostility.

One particularly tough evening, after a day filled with arguments and tears, Sarah and Mike found themselves on their back porch, wondering if they'd made a colossal mistake. That's when Sarah reached for her Bible, turning to a passage that had always brought her comfort:

Genuine affection exhibits patience and kindness. It refrains from jealousy, arrogance, and conceit. Such love avoids disrespecting others, pursues selflessness, maintains composure, and forgives without keeping score of offenses.

As they read these words together, something shifted in their hearts. They realized their calling as Christian stepparents wasn't just about creating a harmonious household (though that would be nice!). It was about embodying Christ's love in a tangible way for their children.

You might think, "That's an interesting story about Sarah and Mike, but how can I relate this to my circumstances?" Don't worry - we're about to explore some actionable techniques to help you manage the complexities of being a stepparent, all while using your spiritual beliefs as a guiding force.

First things first: Prayer Warriors Unite!

Sarah and Mike started each day by praying together for each child by name before the kids woke up. They asked God for wisdom (because, let's face it, some days you need the wisdom of Solomon to figure out who ate the last cookie), patience (oh boy, do you need patience!), and opportunities to show love.

Why not try this? Set your alarm 15 minutes earlier (I know, but trust me on this), and start your day by inviting God into the messiness of your blended family life. You might be surprised at how it changes your perspective and strengthens you for the day ahead.

Next up: One-on-One Time

This one's crucial, folks. Sarah and Mike made it a point to spend individual time with each child, including their stepchildren. This wasn't about grand gestures or expensive outings. Sometimes, it was as simple as Mike shooting hoops with Jake in the driveway or Sarah having a nail painting session with Lily.

The goal? To build personal relationships and create a safe space for open communication. Because let's face it, it's much harder for a kid to see you as the "evil stepparent" when you're cheering them on at their soccer game or listening to them gush about their latest crush.

Family Devotions: More Than Just Reading Bible Stories

Now, I can almost hear some of you groaning. "Family devotions? My kids can barely sit still for dinner, let alone a Bible study!" I get it. But hear me out. Sarah and Mike instituted a weekly family devotion night, and it became a cornerstone of their family life.

The key? They kept it engaging and relevant. They didn't just read a Bible story and call it a day. They discussed how it applied to their lives, shared personal experiences, and sometimes even acted out the stories (picture Mike as a very reluctant Goliath to Jake's enthusiastic David).

These devotion times became a way to build a shared spiritual foundation and create family inside jokes and memories. Plus, they allowed them to address family issues through the lens of faith—a win-win!

Honoring the Past While Moving Forward

This one's especially important for families dealing with loss, whether through death or divorce. Sarah and Mike consciously tried to talk openly about Lily's mother and keep her memory alive. They recognized that honoring the past was crucial for healing and moving forward.

For you, this might mean keeping photos of the children's other parent displayed in the home or talking positively about them (even when it's complicated). It's about showing your stepchildren that loving you doesn't mean forgetting or betraying their other parent.

United We Stand: Presenting a United Front

Okay, this one's a biggie. Sarah and Mike committed to presenting a united front in parenting decisions, always supporting each other in front of the children. They sometimes disagreed behind closed doors (spoiler alert: they didn't). But they made sure to hash out their differences privately and present a unified approach to the kids.

Why is this so important? Because kids, bless their hearts, are master manipulators. They can smell division like sharks smell blood in the water. By presenting a united front, you're giving them the security of clear boundaries and expectations.

Now, I know what some of you might be thinking. "This all sounds great in theory, but what about when the rubber meets the road? What about those tough moments?"

Well, buckle up because we're about to tackle some of the most common challenges Christian stepparents face and how you can approach them with faith and grace.

Challenge #1: The Dreaded "You're Not My Real Mom/Dad"

Ouch. If you have not heard this one, brace yourself because it's probably coming. When Jake first hurled these words at Mike during an argument over bedtime, Mike felt a surge of anger and hurt. Rather than responding reactively, he paused to compose himself. He reflected on the virtues outlined in Galatians, chapter 5, verses 22 and 23, known as the fruits of the Spirit: affection, happiness, tranquility, forbearance, benevolence, virtue, loyalty, mildness, and restraint.

Mike knelt at Jake's eye level and said calmly, "You're right, Jake. I'm not your biological dad. But I love you and am committed to being here for you as your stepdad. I know this is hard for you, and having those feelings is okay. Can we talk about what's bothering you?"

This response, rooted in empathy and self-control, opened the door for a heartfelt conversation that brought Mike and Jake closer together.

The takeaway? When those hurtful words come (and they will), take a breath, remind yourself of God's love for you, and respond with empathy rather than anger. It's not easy, but it can be transformative.

Challenge #2: The Parenting Style Tug-of-War

Sarah and Mike quickly realized they had different approaches to discipline. Sarah tended to be more lenient, while Mike believed in stricter consequences. This difference led to tension between them and confusion for the children.

They turned to Proverbs 22:6 for guidance: "Start children off on the way they should go, and even when they are old, they will not turn from it." They realized their ultimate goal as parents was to guide their children toward a life of faith and good character.

With this in mind, they prayerfully developed a unified parenting approach incorporating nurture and discipline. They agreed on family rules and consequences, explaining the reasoning behind each one to the children. This consistency helped create a sense of security for all the kids and reduced conflicts between Sarah and Mike.

This might mean sitting down with your spouse and conversing honestly about your parenting philosophies. Where do you agree? Where do you differ? How can you find a middle ground that honors both perspectives and, most importantly, provides a stable environment for your children?

Challenge #3: Dealing with Ex-Spouses (A.K.A. The Elephant in the Room)

While Mike didn't have to deal with this issue, Sarah often became frustrated by her ex-husband's inconsistent involvement in Jake and Ethan's lives. The urge to speak ill of him before the kids was strong, but she remembered Jesus' words from Matthew's Gospel, chapter 5, verse 44. This scripture encourages believers to extend compassion to those who oppose them and to pray for individuals who cause them harm.d Christ's teaching from the Gospel of Matthew, chapter 5, verse 44. In this passage, Jesus instructs his followers to show love to their adversaries and offer prayers for those who mistreat them.

Sarah consciously tried to speak respectfully about her ex-husband and encouraged the boys to have a relationship with him. She also committed to praying for him regularly, asking God to work in his heart and life. This approach set a godly example for her children and brought her peace and freedom from bitterness.

Some of you might be dealing with much more difficult ex-spouse situations. Maybe there's been infidelity, abuse, or abandonment. In these cases, it's crucial to seek wisdom from your pastor or a Christian counselor on navigating these waters while protecting your children and honoring God.

Challenge #4: The Loyalty Tug-of-War

Many stepchildren feel caught between their biological

parent and their stepparent, leading to loyalty conflicts. As a Christian stepparent, you might find yourself in situations where your stepchild is reluctant to bond with you out of fear of betraying their biological parent.

For example, Lily initially refused to participate in mother-daughter activities with Sarah because she felt it dishonored her late mother's memory. This can be heartbreaking for a stepparent trying to build a relationship.

To address this:

- Acknowledge and validate the child's feelings

- Reassure them that loving you doesn't mean loving their biological parentless

- Establish a welcoming climate where individuals can openly voice their worries and doubts.

- Pray for wisdom to navigate these delicate emotional waters.

Remember, building these relationships takes time. Don't rush it. Show consistent love and care, and trust God to work in your stepchild's heart.

Challenge #5: Blending Different Faith Backgrounds

In some blended families, children may come from different faith backgrounds. This can create tension, especially around religious practices and beliefs.

For instance, if Mike's late wife wasn't a believer, Lily might resist participating in family devotions or attending church. This presents a challenge in creating a unified Christian household.

Here are some possible approaches:

- Be patient and lead by example rather than forcing participation

- Find ways to incorporate faith discussions naturally into daily life

- Pray for opportunities to share your faith in a non-threatening way

- Seek guidance from your pastor on how to navigate this sensitively

Your primary focus should be cultivating a space that encourages unrestricted exploration of faith and regularly demonstrates godly love. This approach requires patience, understanding, and a lot of prayer, but it can lead to beautiful transformations in your blended family.

Challenge #6: Managing Financial Stress

Blended families often face unique financial challenges, such as child support payments, different financial habits, or resentment over spending on stepchildren. These issues can strain the marital relationship and impact the entire family dynamic.

To address this:

- Pray together about your finances.

- Be transparent with each other about financial obligations and expectations.

- Create an all-encompassing monetary strategy that addresses every family member's individual needs and financial obligations.

- Consider seeking Christian financial counseling if needed.

Remember, all resources ultimately belong to God (Psalm 24:1). You're stewards of His resources, called to manage them wisely for the benefit of your entire family.

Challenge #7: Navigating Grief and Loss

Both adults and children in blended families may be dealing with unresolved grief - whether from divorce, the death of a parent, or the loss of the "ideal" family they once envisioned.

For example, Jake and Ethan might act out not because they dislike Mike but because they're grieving the loss of their dream that their biological parents would reconcile.

As a Christian stepparent:

- Recognize that grief is a process and allow space for it

- Encourage open expression of feelings

- Consider Christian counseling for family members struggling with grief

- Use this as an opportunity to teach about God's comfort in times of loss

Remember, Jesus was well-acquainted with grief (Isaiah 53:3). He understands what you and your family are going through and offers comfort and healing.

Challenge #8: Holiday Havoc

Blended families often face unique difficulties during festive seasons and when observing family customs. Individual members might have varying anticipations or sentimental connections to particular rituals.

To handle this:

- Be willing to compromise and create new traditions

- Involve all family members in decision-making about holidays

- Be flexible and understanding about time spent with other biological parents during holidays

- Use holidays to teach about Christian values like generosity and family love

Remember, the most important thing about holidays is not the specific traditions but the love and connection shared. Whatever your celebrations look like, create a warm, loving atmosphere.

Challenge #9: Dealing with Outside Judgment

Unfortunately, blended families sometimes face judgment or lack of understanding from others, even within the church community. This can be hurtful and isolating.

To cope with this:

- Remember that God's opinion matters most

- Seek out supportive friends and family members

- Consider starting a support group for blended families in your church

- Use these experiences to teach your children about not judging others

Recall Christ's teaching in the Gospel of John, chapter 13, verses 34 and 35. He instructs his followers with a fresh directive: show mutual love. He emphasizes that they should love each other like he has loved them. Jesus explains that this display of love will be the distinguishing mark by which others recognize his faithful followers.

Challenge #10: Maintaining Your Marriage Amidst Stepfamily Stress

With so much focus on the children and managing family dynamics, it's easy for the couple's relationship to take a backseat. However, a strong marriage is crucial for a healthy, blended family.

To strengthen your marriage:

- Prioritize regular date nights

- Pray together daily

- Seek marriage counseling if needed

- Remember that your marriage is the foundation of your blended family

As you navigate these challenges, remember that you're not alone. God has called you to this role for a reason, and He will equip you with the tools you need to succeed. Your role as a Christian stepparent is a high calling, and with God's help, you can rise to the challenge and create a home filled with love, grace, and the peace of Christ.

Here are some final thoughts to encourage you on your journey:

1. Embrace your calling with courage and hope. The road may not always be easy, but with God's guidance and the support of your church community, you can create a loving, Christ-centered blended family that reflects God's heart for adoption and unconditional love.

2. Commit daily prayer for each family member, asking God for wisdom, patience, and opportunities to show love.

3. Initiate regular family devotion times to build a shared spiritual foundation.

4. Seek support from other Christian stepparents or a blended family support group at your church.

5. Be intentional about building individual relationships with each of your stepchildren.

6. Regularly communicate with your spouse about parenting decisions and family dynamics, ensuring you present a united front.

Remember, you're not just building a family; you're creating a legacy of love that can impact future generations. Your blended family has the potential to be a powerful testimony of God's love and grace.

So, dear Christian stepparent, take heart. Yes, the journey is challenging, but it's also gratifying. With each act of love, word of encouragement, and moment of patience, you're showing your family—and the world—what God's love looks like in action.

And when you feel overwhelmed (because those days will come), remember the promise in Philippians 1:6: "Being confident of this, that he who began a good work in you will carry it on to completion until the day of Christ Jesus." God has called you to this role and will see you through.

Your blended family is a beautiful, messy, excellent work in progress. And guess what? God specializes in works in progress. He still needs to finish you and certainly still needs to finish your family. So keep loving, praying, trying, and watching in wonder as God weaves your blended family into a masterpiece of His grace.

CHAPTER ONE

The Biblical Foundation for Stepparenting

The divine protects those without fathers and women who have lost their husbands. The Lord also shows compassion to newcomers living in your community, providing for their basic needs of sustenance and attire.

You never expected to be here, did you? Sitting on the edge of your bed, staring at a wedding photo that now feels like it belongs to someone else's life. The path that led you to becoming a stepparent wasn't one you planned, but here you are – about to embark on one of your life's most challenging and potentially rewarding journeys.

As you contemplate the road ahead, you might feel excitement, apprehension, and maybe even a touch of fear. That's okay. It's completely normal. Stepparenting is no small task, and it comes with its own unique set of challenges. But before we dive into the practical aspects of navigating this new family dynamic, let's take a moment to ground ourselves in something more profound – a biblical foundation for stepparenting.

You might wonder, "Does the Bible even address stepparenting?" While the term "stepparent" doesn't appear in scripture, the concept of caring for children who aren't biologically yours is woven throughout God's Word. It's at the heart of God's character and His plan for humanity.

God's Heart for Blended Families

Let's start with a story you're familiar with but may not have considered from this angle.

Imagine yourself in ancient Egypt, over 3,000 years ago. The air is thick with the day's heat, and the Nile River flows steadily nearby. A young Hebrew woman named Jochebed clutches a small basket, her heart pounding with fear and hope. Inside that basket is her three-month-old son – a child she can no longer hide from Pharaoh's cruel decree that all Hebrew boys be thrown into the Nile.

With trembling hands, she places the basket among the reeds at the river's edge, whispering a prayer for her baby's safety. Little does she know that God is about to weave together a blended family that will change the course of history.

You know how the story unfolds. Pharaoh's daughter discovers the baby, her heart melting at his cries. Despite knowing he's a Hebrew child – one condemned to death by her own father's decree – she makes a choice. A choice to love. A choice to protect. A choice to parent a child who isn't her own.

This is Moses' story, but it's yours in many ways. Like Pharaoh's daughter, you're choosing to love a child who isn't biologically yours. You're stepping into a role that requires courage, compassion, and much faith.

The story of Moses isn't an isolated incident in scripture. Scripture contains numerous instances demonstrating divine concern for non-traditional family units.

1. The notion of welcoming individuals as family members is fundamental to our spiritual connection with the divine. As stated in Ephesians' first chapter, verse five, the Creator predetermined our inclusion into God's family through the work of Jesus Christ. " When you choose to love and care for a child who isn't biologically yours, you're reflecting the very heart of God.

2. Jesus' family structure: Remember, Jesus was raised by a stepfather. Joseph chose to marry Mary and raise Jesus as his own despite the societal scandal and personal sacrifice it entailed.

3. God's love for all children: Throughout scripture, we see God's concern for orphans and vulnerable children. Psalm 68:5- 6 describes God as "A father to the fatherless, a defender of widows," who "sets the lonely in families."

As you embark on this stepparenting journey, take comfort in knowing you're participating in a divine pattern reflecting God's heart for family, adoption, and sacrificial love.

Biblical Examples of Stepparenting

Now, let's examine some specific biblical examples of stepparenting. These stories can inspire and provide practical wisdom for your journey.

Joseph and Jesus

Imagine yourself as a humble woodworker living in the town of Nazareth. You're betrothed to a youthful woman called Mary. Your life seems set on a predictable course – until everything changes. Mary is pregnant, and the child isn't yours. What do you do?

This was Joseph's dilemma; his response provides a powerful model for stepparents today. Despite his initial doubts and fears, Joseph embraced his role as Jesus' earthly father. He protected Mary and Jesus from societal scorn, fled to Egypt to escape Herod's wrath, and later raised Jesus in the carpentry trade.

Joseph's example teaches us several key lessons:

1. Commitment: Joseph committed to his role as a father,

regardless of biological ties.

2. Protection: He prioritized the safety and well-being of his blended family.

3. *Involvement:* Joseph was involved in Jesus' upbringing, teaching him a trade.

As a stepparent, you can emulate Joseph's commitment, protection, and involvement in your stepchildren's lives.

Moses and His Adoptive Family

We've already touched on Moses' story, but let's delve deeper. Moses was raised in Pharaoh's household, effectively becoming the adopted son of Pharaoh's daughter. Yet, he never forgot his Hebrew heritage, eventually choosing to align himself with his biological people.

This story highlights an important truth for stepfamilies: Honoring biological and stepfamily ties is possible. Your stepchildren don't have to choose between their biological parent and you – there's room in their hearts for both.

Mordecai and Esther

The Book of Esther provides another powerful example of stepparenting. After Esther's parents died, her cousin Mordecai took her as his daughter. Mordecai's guidance and support ultimately positioned Esther to save the entire Jewish people from genocide.

Mordecai's example teaches us:

1. Guidance: Stepparents can provide crucial guidance and wisdom.

2. Support: Your support can empower your stepchildren to fulfill their potential.

3. Advocacy: Like Mordecai, you can be a powerful advocate for your stepchildren.

Christian Principles in Stepparenting

As we reflect on these biblical examples, several fundamental Christian principles emerge that can guide us in our stepparenting journey:

Unconditional Love

Genuine affection shows forbearance and benevolence. It avoids jealousy, bragging, and arrogance. This love respects others, is selfless, maintains composure, and forgives without keeping score of offenses.

Unconditional love is at the heart of Christian parenting – and stepparenting is no exception. This love isn't based on biology, shared experiences, or reciprocation. It's a choice to love, regardless of circumstances or responses.

Imagine for a moment that you're sitting at the dinner table with your blended family. Your stepson, a teenager struggling to adjust to the new family dynamic, has just said something hurtful. Your initial reaction might be anger or frustration. But what if, in that moment, you chose to respond with patience and kindness instead?

Unconditional love doesn't mean ignoring misbehavior or never setting boundaries. But it does mean consistently choosing to act in the best interest of your stepchild, even when it's complicated.

Forgiveness and Grace

Show gentleness and empathy in your interactions with others. Extend forgiveness to one another, mirroring the divine pardon God has granted you through Christ.

Blended families often have emotional baggage – past hurts, resentments, and fears. Forgiveness and grace are essential tools for navigating these complex emotional landscapes.

Consider this scenario: Your stepdaughter consistently pushes you away, clinging to the hope that her biological parents will reconcile. It hurts, and it's tempting to withdraw or respond with coldness. But what if you chose to extend grace instead? To forgive the rejection and continue to offer love and support?

Forgiveness doesn't mean forgetting or excusing hurtful behavior. Instead, it's a decision to release the right to retaliate and to continue loving despite the hurt. It's a powerful force that can gradually soften hearts and heal relationships.

Sacrificial Service

Even Jesus, the Son of Man, arrived not to receive service but to offer it. His purpose was to sacrifice himself as payment to liberate many.

At its core, Christian parenting – including stepparenting – is about sacrificial service. It's about putting the needs of your stepchildren above your comfort or preferences.

This might look like:

- Adjusting your schedule to attend your stepchild's school events

- Learning to appreciate your stepchild's interests, even if they're different from your own

- Patiently building trust over time, even when progress seems slow

Remember the story of Jesus washing His disciples' feet? As a stepparent, you're called to this same kind of humble, selfless service. It's not always easy, but in this place of sacrificial love, real bonds are formed, and lives are changed.

Practical Application

As we wrap up this chapter, let's focus on some practical ways you can apply these biblical principles in your stepparenting journey:

1. Prioritize relationship-building: Make intentional efforts to spend one-on-one time with your stepchildren. This

could be as simple as a weekly ice cream date or a shared hobby. The key is consistency and genuine interest in their lives.

2. Practice active listening: Tune in when your stepchildren speak. Try to understand their words and the emotions and needs behind them. This empathetic listening can go a long way in building trust and connection.

3. Extend grace daily: Look for opportunities to extend grace in everyday situations. Did your stepchild forget to do their chores again? Instead of immediately punishing, consider using it as a teaching moment, offering forgiveness and gentle guidance.

4. Demonstrate the practice of pardoning others: During inevitable disagreements, be swift to forgive and ready to seek forgiveness when you're at fault. Your example can set the tone for how your blended family handles disagreements.

5. Serve sacrificially: Look for ways to serve your stepchildren that might not come naturally to you. This could mean attending a concert of music you don't particularly enjoy or learning to play a video game your stepchild loves. These acts of service speak volumes

about your commitment and love.

As you implement these principles, remember that change often happens slowly. There may be days when you feel like you need to make progress. In those moments, please return to the biblical examples we've discussed. Remember Joseph's patient commitment, Mordecai's steadfast support, and the unconditional love of your Heavenly Father.

You're not just building a family but participating in God's redemptive work. Every act of love, every extension of grace, and every moment of sacrificial service is a brushstroke in a beautiful picture of restoration and hope.

As we move into the next chapter, where we'll explore stepparents' unique challenges, hold onto this biblical foundation.

Let it be an anchor for your soul and a guide for your actions.

Remember, you're not alone in this journey. The God who sets the lonely in families is with you every step of the way.

CHAPTER TWO

Understanding the Stepfamily Dynamics

While enjoying your early cup of coffee at home and browsing social networking sites, you become aware of a growing trend in posts showcasing non-traditional family units. It's not just your imagination – stepfamilies are becoming more prevalent in modern society. In fact, according to recent statistics, about 40% of married couples with children in the United States are step-couples, and 30% of all children are growing up in a stepfamily.

These numbers might make you feel less alone in your journey, but they don't necessarily make the challenges any more accessible. As you reflect on your situation, you realize that understanding the unique dynamics of stepfamilies is crucial for navigating this new chapter in your life.

Let's explore the world of stepfamilies through the story of the Johnsons, a blended family trying to find its footing in this complex landscape.

Meet Sarah, a divorced mother of two teenagers, Jack (15) and Emma (13). She recently married Tom, a widower with a 10-year-old son, Max. As they embark on their new life together, they quickly realize that merging two families is far more challenging than initially thought.

Common Challenges in Stepfamilies

1. Loyalty Conflicts

It's a lazy Sunday afternoon, and you're lounging on the couch with your new stepchildren, trying to decide on a movie to watch. Suddenly, your stepdaughter Emma blurts out, "I wish Dad were here. He always knows the best movies to pick."

You feel a pang in your chest. This is not the first time Emma has expressed her longing for her biological father; you know it won't be the last. This is a classic example of a loyalty conflict—a common challenge in stepfamilies.

Sarah notices the hurt look on your face and gently intervenes. "Emma, honey, I know you miss your dad. It's okay to feel that way. But let's try to make Tom feel included, too.

He may have some great movie suggestions we haven't thought of.

Emma nods reluctantly, and you appreciate Sarah's effort to bridge the gap. But you can't help wondering if you'll ever be accepted as part of the family.

Loyalty conflicts arise when children are torn between their biological parents and stepparents. They might worry that enjoying time with you means betraying their other parent. It's a delicate balance; navigating these emotions requires patience and understanding from everyone involved.

2. *Establishing Authority*

A few days later, you are arguing with Jack about his curfew. "You're not my real dad!" he shouts, slamming his bedroom door in your face. You stand there, feeling a mix of frustration and helplessness.

Establishing authority as a stepparent is one of your trickiest challenges. You want to be involved in parenting decisions but are acutely aware that you're stepping into a pre-existing family dynamic. How much authority should you assert? When should you step back and let Sarah take the lead?

As you and Sarah discuss the incident later that night, she suggests, "Maybe we need to have a family meeting to discuss house rules and expectations. It might help if the kids see us presenting a united front."

You nod, realizing that clear communication and consistency are vital in establishing your role within the family.

3. Dealing with Ex-Partners

The following weekend, you're preparing for Max's soccer game when Tom's late ex-wife, Lisa, shows up unexpectedly. She insists on driving Max to the game, disrupting your plans. You feel a surge of irritation, but you bite your tongue, knowing that maintaining a civil relationship with ex-partners is crucial for the children's well-being.

As you watch Lisa drive away with Max, Sarah squeezes your hand. "I know it's not easy," she says. "But remember, we're all on the same team regarding the kids."

Dealing with ex-partners is often an unavoidable part of stepfamily life. It requires maturity, patience, and a willingness to put the children's needs first, even when challenging.

The Stepfamily Life Cycle

As you navigate these challenges, it's helpful to understand that stepfamilies typically go through several stages of development. Recognizing where you are in this cycle can provide valuable perspective and hope for the future.

1. *Formation Stage*

Cast your mind back to the early days of your relationship with Sarah. Everything seemed perfect – you were in love, and bringing your families together filled you with excitement. This honeymoon phase is typical of the formation stage.

You remember your first family outing to the local fair. The kids seemed to get along well, laughing and enjoying the rides together. You and Sarah exchanged hopeful glances, thinking, "This might work perfectly."

But as the weeks went by, reality began to set in. The children's initial politeness gave way to sibling rivalries and power struggles. You found yourself constantly navigating unfamiliar territory, figuring out your place in this new family dynamic.

High hopes and expectations characterize the formation stage, but it's also a time of significant adjustment for everyone involved. It's normal to feel overwhelmed and uncertain during this period.

2. *Adjustment Stage*

Fast-forward a few months, and you find yourself in the middle of the adjustment stage. This is where the real work of blending your families begins.

You're sitting at the dinner table, listening to Max and Emma argue over who gets the last slice of pizza. Jack is sulking because he wants to eat in his room, and Sarah looks like she's about to lose her patience. It's a far cry from the harmonious family dinners you once envisioned.

But then something unexpected happens. Max offers to split the last slice with Emma, and Jack reluctantly joins the conversation, sharing a funny story from school. It's a small moment, but it gives you hope that you're making progress, however slowly.

The adjustment stage is often the longest and most challenging phase of stepfamily development. It involves negotiation, compromise, and learning to live together as a new unit. Patience is critical during this stage, as it can take years for a stepfamily to adjust fully.

3. *Resolution Stage*

While you're not quite there yet, you can see glimpses of the resolution stage for your family. It's the light at the end of the tunnel, the stage where stepfamilies finally find their groove.

You imagine a future family gathering where inside jokes flow freely, where the kids seek advice from both you and Sarah without hesitation, and where the word "step" becomes less and less relevant in your daily interactions.

The resolution stage doesn't mean that all problems disappear, but rather that the family has developed effective ways of dealing with challenges together. It's a stage of acceptance, stability, and a strong family identity.

Unique Roles in a Stepfamily

As you reflect on your journey, you realize that each member of your blended family plays a unique role, each with its challenges and responsibilities.

1. Stepparent

Your role as a stepparent is the most complex and least defined in the family structure. You're not quite a parent but more than just a friend. It would help if you were supportive without overstepping authority without being overbearing.

You remember the first time Emma came to you for advice about a problem at school. It wasn't a groundbreaking issue, but the fact that she sought you out made you feel accepted and valued. These small moments of connection are what make the challenges of stepparenting worthwhile.

As a stepparent, your primary tasks are to:

- Build a relationship with your stepchildren at their pace

- Support your partner in their parenting decisions

- Find your place within the existing family dynamic without trying to replace the biological parent

2. *Biological Parent*

Sarah's role as the biological parent comes with its challenges. She's the bridge between you and her children, balancing everyone's needs and emotions.

You've seen Sarah struggle with guilt – guilt for the divorce, guilt for bringing a new person into her children's lives, guilt for sometimes siding with you over her kids. It's a heavy burden to bear.

But you've also seen her strength and resilience. For example, Sarah organized a family study session when Jack struggled in school. She ensured you were involved, gently encouraging Jack to accept your help with his math homework.

The biological parent's role involves:

- Facilitating a relationship between the stepparent and the children

- Maintaining open communication with the ex-partner for the children's sake

- Balancing attention between the new spouse and the

children

3. *Stepchild*

Finally, the children – Jack, Emma, and Max – each deal with their complex emotions about this new family arrangement.

You've watched them struggle with divided loyalties, uncertainty about their place in the family, and the challenge of adapting to new rules and expectations. But you've also seen their resilience and capacity for love.

Like the time Max drew a family portrait for a school project. He included everyone – you, Sarah, Jack, Emma, and even his late mother. It was a powerful reminder that children have an incredible ability to expand their concept of family.

The role of a stepchild includes:

- Adjusting to new family dynamics and relationships

- Dealing with complex emotions about the changes in their family structure

- Learning to balance relationships with biological parents and stepparents

As you ponder these roles and the journey your family has been on, you realize that while the challenges of stepfamily life are real, so are the rewards. Every small victory, every moment of connection, brings you one step closer to becoming a strong, cohesive family unit.

Remember, there's no one-size-fits-all solution for blending families. What works for the Johnsons might not work for your family, and that's okay. The key is approaching the process with patience, understanding, and a willingness to adapt.

Here are some key takeaways to help you navigate your stepfamily journey:

- Clear exchanges are vital: Encourage transparent, sincere conversations among all household members. Create a climate where each individual believes their input is valued and their opinions are given due consideration.

- Be patient: Building strong family bonds takes time. Don't expect instant harmony – celebrate small victories and learn from setbacks.

- Maintain realistic expectations: Perfect families don't exist, blended or otherwise. Embrace your stepfamily's unique dynamics and focus on progress, not perfection.

- Pursue assistance: Be proactive in connecting with allies, community groups, or qualified therapists familiar with the distinct issues faced by non-traditional family units.

- Prioritize your relationship: While focusing on the children is essential, don't neglect your partnership. A strong couple relationship provides a stable foundation for the entire family.

As you set aside your device and drain the last of your cooled beverage, you experience a fresh wave of motivation. While recognizing these family complexities doesn't eliminate obstacles, it equips you with crucial strategies to tackle them. Remember, others share similar experiences on this path. You can cultivate a resilient and joyful non-traditional household through perseverance, empathy, and affection.

In the next chapter, we'll explore practical strategies for building solid relationships within your stepfamily, drawing on our insights about stepfamily dynamics.

Remember, every family's journey is unique, but with persistence and compassion, you can create a loving and harmonious home for all members of your blended family.

CHAPTER THREE

Cultivating Love in Your Blended Family

You never thought you'd be here. Standing in the kitchen of a house that doesn't quite feel like home, surrounded by children who aren't biologically yours, married to someone who comes with a whole history you weren't part of. Yet here you are, a stepparent, trying to navigate the complex waters of a blended family.

Meet Sarah. She was once where you are now, feeling like an outsider in her home, unsure of her place in this new family dynamic. Let's follow her journey as she learns to cultivate love in her blended family, transforming from an uncertain newcomer to an integral part of a loving, cohesive unit.

Sarah met Tom when she least expected it. They found each other in their early forties after their first marriages had ended. Tom came with two children: Lily, a precocious 12-year-old, and Max, a quiet 9-year-old. Sarah had no children, and the prospect of instant motherhood was exciting and terrifying.

The wedding was beautiful, but the honeymoon phase didn't last long. Reality set in quickly as Sarah moved into Tom's house, now technically hers too, but still feeling like someone else's space. Photos of Tom's ex-wife were tucked away in drawers, but her presence lingered in the children's mannerisms, the way the house was organized, and the family traditions Sarah knew nothing about.

Those first few months were a whirlwind of adjustment. Sarah tried her best to fit in, make herself useful, and show Tom's children that she cared. But more often than not, she felt like an intruder. Lily would give her the cold shoulder, Max would retreat to his room whenever she tried to engage him, and even Tom seemed distant at times, caught between his love for Sarah and his loyalty to his kids.

One night, after a particularly tense family dinner in which Lily stormed off, and Max barely spoke, Sarah was sitting on the back porch, tears streaming down her face. She wondered if she had made a terrible mistake. Maybe she wasn't cut out for this. Maybe love wasn't enough to bridge the gap between her and these children who didn't want her here.

But as she sat there, feeling more alone than ever, she heard the back door open. It was Tom. He sat beside her, took her hand, and said, "I know this is hard. But we're in this together. We'll figure it out."

That moment was a turning point for Sarah. She realized that cultivating love in a blended family wasn't about forcing relationships or trying to replace anyone. It was about patience, understanding, and, most importantly, teamwork with her spouse. From that night on, Sarah and Tom committed to nurturing their marriage while also working on building bonds with the children.

Nurturing Your Marriage

Sarah and Tom's first step was to prioritize their relationship. They realized that a strong foundation between them was crucial for the stability of their blended family. Here's what they did:

1. Prioritizing couple time: They instituted a weekly date night. Every Friday, no matter what, they would go out, just the two of them. Sometimes, it was dinner at a nice restaurant; other times, it was just a walk in the park or a movie at home after the kids were in bed. The important thing was that it was their time, free from distractions and focused solely on each other.

2. Supporting each other's parenting efforts: They started having regular check-ins about the kids. Tom would share insights about Lily and Max's personalities, likes and dislikes, struggles and triumphs. Sarah would offer her observations and ideas. Together, they'd strategize handling various situations, from homework struggles to

behavioral issues.

3. Presenting a united front was the most challenging but crucial aspect. They agreed that even if they disagreed on a parenting decision, they would support each other in front of the kids. Any differences would be discussed privately. This helped prevent the kids from playing one parent against the other and showed them that Tom and Sarah were a team.

As you navigate your blended family situation, remember these key points:

- Your marriage is the foundation of your blended family. Prioritize it.

- Regular, uninterrupted couple time is essential.

- Support each other's parenting efforts, even when you disagree.

- Present a united front to the children.

- Communicate openly and honestly with each other about challenges and successes.

With their marriage on solid ground, Sarah felt more confident in her role as a stepmother. However, building relationships with Lily and Max was still a challenge. She knew it would take time and patience but was committed to making it work.

Bonding with Stepchildren

Sarah's approach to bonding with Lily and Max was gradual and respectful. She understood that she couldn't force a relationship but could create opportunities for connection. Here's how she went about it:

1. Building trust gradually: Sarah made a point of being consistently present and supportive without being pushy. She'd ask about their day, offer homework help if they wanted, and always follow through on her promises. Sarah was there cheering from the sidelines when Lily had a big soccer game. When Max needed help with a science project, Sarah offered her assistance but let him take the lead.

2. Finding common interests: Sarah paid attention to what the kids enjoyed and sought ways to connect over shared interests. She discovered Lily loved baking, so she invited her to help make cookies one afternoon. It started awkwardly, with Lily barely speaking, but the tension began to ease as they worked side by side, measuring

ingredients and decorating the cookies. By the end of the afternoon, Lily was laughing as they tried to outdo each other with increasingly elaborate cookie designs. With Max, the connection came through books. Sarah noticed that Max always had his nose in a fantasy novel. She had not read much in that genre but decided to try it. She picked up the first book in the series Max was reading and started conversations about the characters and plot. Max was initially surprised that Sarah was interested, but soon, they started having animated discussions about the magical world in the books.

3. Respecting boundaries: Sarah was careful not to overstep. She never tried to replace the children's mother or force affection. When Lily was having a bad day and wanted to be left alone, Sarah respected that. She'd say, "I'm here if you need anything," and give Lily her space. With Max, who was sometimes uncomfortable with physical affection from Sarah, she found other ways to show she cared, like leaving encouraging notes in his lunchbox or giving him a thumbs up when he did well on a test.

As you work on bonding with your stepchildren, keep these points in mind:

- Trust takes time. Be patient and consistent in your efforts.

- Look for common interests as a way to connect.

- Respect boundaries, and don't try to force affection.

- Be supportive without trying to replace the biological parent.

- Celebrate small victories – every positive interaction is a step forward.

Sarah's efforts didn't lead to an immediate transformation, but things began to change slowly, almost imperceptibly at first. Lily started inviting Sarah out to bake together more often, and Max began recommending books for Sarah to read. Of course, there were still challenging days, but the overall trend was positive.

As Sarah's relationships with Lily and Max improved, she noticed another issue that needed attention: the siblings' relationship.

Fostering Sibling Relationships

Lily and Max had a somewhat contentious relationship, typical of many siblings with a three-year age gap. However, the stress of the divorce and remarriage exacerbated their conflicts. Sarah and Tom realized that fostering a positive sibling relationship was crucial for family harmony. Here's how they approached it:

1. Encouraging empathy: Sarah and Tom consciously tried to help Lily and Max see things from each other's perspective. When Lily complained about Max being annoying, Sarah gently reminded her of times when she was younger and looked up to her older cousins. When Max is frustrated by Lily's moodiness, Tom explains that being a preteen is challenging and that Lily is dealing with many changes. One day, after a particularly nasty argument between the siblings, Sarah sat them down and asked each to write a letter from the other's point of view. Lily had to write as if she were Max and Max as if he were Lily. The exercise was initially met with eye-rolls, but as they read their letters aloud, both kids were surprised by how well they understood each other's feelings.

2. Creating shared experiences: Sarah and Tom looked for activities that Lily and Max could enjoy together. They started a family game night every Saturday, rotating who got to choose the game. They also enrolled both kids in a local youth theater program. Neither Lily nor Max had done theater before, but they loved it. Working together on the school play gave them a shared goal and plenty of inside jokes. During summer vacation, the family took a camping trip. Being in nature, away from their usual distractions, provided many opportunities for Lily and Max to work together and have fun. They collaborated on setting up the tent, gathering firewood, and even creating their scavenger hunt in the woods. By the end of the trip, their bickering had noticeably decreased.

3. Mediating conflicts reasonably: When conflicts did arise, Sarah and Tom handled them impartially. They established a family meeting format where everyone could speak without interruption. They taught the kids to use "I feel" statements instead of accusations, and they always tried to guide Lily and Max toward finding their solutions rather than imposing one. One memorable instance was when Lily and Max fought over the family tablet's use. Instead of setting a schedule, Sarah and Tom had the kids work together to create a fair system. After

some negotiation (and a bit of bribing), Lily and Max devised a points system where they could earn tablet time through chores and good behavior. Not only did this solve the immediate problem, but it gave the siblings practice in compromise and collaboration.

As you work on fostering positive sibling relationships in your blended family, remember:

- Encourage empathy by helping siblings see things from each other's perspective.

- Create opportunities for positive shared experiences.

- Teach and model fair conflict resolution skills.

- Allow siblings to work together to solve problems when possible.

- Celebrate moments of sibling harmony and cooperation.

Over time, Sarah began to see fundamental changes in her family. A growing sense of warmth and belonging gradually replaced the tension that had once filled the house. There were still challenges – blending a family is never a smooth or finished process – but Sarah no longer felt like an outsider.

One day, about two years after the wedding, Sarah had a

moment that made her realize how far they'd come. She was in the kitchen, helping Max with his math homework while a batch of Lily's favorite cookies baked in the oven. Tom came home from work, kissed Sarah, and started chatting with the kids about their day. As Sarah looked around at her family, she felt a wave of love and contentment. This was home. These were her people. They had cultivated this love together through patience, effort, and unwavering commitment.

Just then, Lily came bouncing into the kitchen, sniffing the air appreciatively. "Ooh, you made the cookies! Thanks, Mom!" she said casually, reaching for one. Then she froze, realizing what she'd said. Sarah felt her heart skip a beat. It was the first time Lily had called her Mom.

For a moment, everyone was silent. Then Lily shrugged, grabbed a cookie, and said, "Well, you are, aren't you? My other Mom." And with that, she skipped out of the room, leaving Sarah with tears and a smile.

That night, as Sarah and Tom sat on the porch – the same porch where, two years earlier, Sarah had cried and questioned everything – they reflected on their journey. "It hasn't been easy," Tom said, squeezing Sarah's hand. "But it's been worth it."

Sarah nodded, thinking of all the small moments that had led to this point:

- The family game nights

- The shared jokes

- The hard conversations

- The gradual building of trust and love

"It has," she agreed. We've created something beautiful here."

Remember Sarah's story as you continue on your journey of blending a family. Remember that love in a blended family doesn't happen overnight. It's cultivated daily through small acts of kindness, persistence in facing challenges, and respect for each other's feelings and boundaries. It's nurtured in the strength of your marriage, the bonds you build with your stepchildren, and the relationships you foster between siblings.

There will be hard days. Sometimes, you feel like an outsider when you question whether you're making any progress at all. Take a deep breath in those moments and remind yourself that you're playing the long game. No matter how small, every positive interaction is a step in the right direction. Every challenge you overcome together makes your family stronger.

Remember these key points as you cultivate love in your

blended family:

- Prioritize your marriage. A strong partnership between you and your spouse is the foundation for everything else.

- Build relationships with your stepchildren gradually and respectfully. Look for common interests and ways to connect.

- Foster positive sibling relationships by encouraging empathy, creating shared experiences, and teaching fair conflict resolution.

- Be patient. Building a blended family takes time.

- Celebrate the small victories along the way.

Your non-traditional family unit can become a rich source of affection, encouragement, and happiness. While challenges will arise, you can forge a caring household that reflects your distinct family identity through perseverance, empathy, and dedication.As Sarah did, you, too, can transform from feeling like an outsider to being an integral, beloved part of your blended family.

As you move forward, remember that effective communication is critical to maintaining and strengthening the love you're cultivating. The next chapter will explore strategies for fostering open, honest, and respectful communication within your blended family.

CHAPTER FOUR

Communicating with Grace and Truth

Have you had the experience of attending a live performance by a complete orchestral ensemble? The way each instrument blends seamlessly with the others creates a harmonious masterpiece that moves the soul. Now, imagine your family as that orchestra. Each member has a unique voice and an instrument to play. When everyone works together, listening and responding in tune, the result can be as beautiful and powerful as any symphony.

But let's be honest—family life isn't always a perfect performance. Sometimes, it's more like a cacophony of competing sounds, each person trying to be heard over the others. That's where effective communication comes in. The conductor brings order to the chaos, allowing each family member's voice to shine while creating a harmonious whole.

You're about to embark on a journey to transform your

family's communication from discord to harmony. Along the way, you'll meet the Johnsons, a family much like yours struggling to find their rhythm. Through their story, you'll discover practical tools to enhance your listening skills, express your needs clearly, and resolve conflicts with grace and truth.

The Johnson Family's Crescendo of Chaos

It's a typical Tuesday evening at the Johnson household. Mom, Sarah, is trying to coordinate dinner plans while fielding work calls. Dad, Mike, has just walked in the door, his mind still buzzing with unfinished office projects. Fourteen-year-old Emma is sprawled on the couch, engrossed in her phone and pointedly ignoring her younger brother, ten-year-old Ethan, who's bugging her about a video game.

The tension in the air is palpable, like an orchestra warming up before a performance—each instrument playing its tune, oblivious to the others. Sarah sighs, feeling the familiar weight of frustration settling on her shoulders. She loves her family dearly, but lately, it feels like they're all speaking different languages.

"Emma, can you please set the table?" Sarah calls out, balancing her phone between her ear and shoulder as she stirs a pot on the stove.

Emma doesn't even look up from her device. "In a minute, Mom. I'm in the middle of something."

"Now, please," Sarah insists, her voice sharpening with irritation.

Mike walks into the kitchen, loosening his tie. "Rough day?" he asks, giving Sarah a quick peck on the cheek.

"You have no idea," Sarah replies, pointing at Emma, who's still glued to her phone. "A little help would be nice."

Mike nods, then turns to Emma. "You heard your mother. Set the table now."

Emma rolls her eyes dramatically. "Fine," she huffs, stomping towards the kitchen.

Meanwhile, Ethan abandons his attempts to engage Emma and tugs on Mike's sleeve. "Dad, can we play that new game after dinner? You promised!"

Mike runs a hand through his hair, looking torn. "I don't know, buddy. I've got a lot of work to catch up on..."

"But you promised!" Ethan wails, his voice rising in pitch.

And just like that, the Johnson household erupts into a cacophony of raised voices, slammed cabinets, and hurt feelings. It's a far cry from the harmonious family life they all long for.

Learning to Listen: The First Notes of Harmony

As the dust settles from their chaotic evening, Sarah and Mike sit at the kitchen table long after the kids go to bed. They're exhausted, discouraged, and wondering how they've gotten to this point.

"We can't go on like this," Sarah says softly, cradling a mug of tea between her hands. "Something has to change."

Mike nods, his usual confident demeanor replaced by a look of vulnerability. "I know. But where do we even start?"

As it turns out, the answer begins with a simple yet profound shift: learning to listen genuinely.

The next day, Sarah decides to practice this with Emma. Instead of immediately reacting to her daughter's moody behavior, she takes a deep breath and approaches Emma with an open heart.

"Hey, sweetie," Sarah says, sitting on the edge of Emma's

bed. "I feel like we've been butting heads a lot lately. I'd love to understand what's going on with you. Can we talk?"

Emma looks up, surprised by her mother's gentle tone. For a moment, she's silent as if weighing whether it's safe to open up. Then, hesitantly, she begins to speak.

"I just... I feel like everyone's always telling me what to do," Emma confesses. "At school, at home... I never get to make my own decisions."

Sarah feels a pang in her heart. She wants to jump in, explain, and fix things but remembers her commitment to listen. Instead, she nods encouragingly, maintaining eye contact with Emma.

"That sounds frustrating," Sarah says softly. "Can you tell me more about that?"

As Emma continues to share, Sarah practices active listening. She empathizes with Emma's emotions, even when she disagrees with her daughter's perspective. She asks clarifying questions to ensure she understands:

"So, when I ask you to set the table, it feels like just another demand on top of everything else?"

And she validates Emma's feelings:

"I can see why you'd feel overwhelmed and want some control over your life."

To Sarah's amazement, the simple act of genuinely listening begins to soften the tension between them. Emma's defensive posture relaxes, and she even manages a small smile.

"Thanks for listening, Mom," Emma says. "I... I didn't think you'd understand."

Sarah reaches out and squeezes Emma's hand. "I'm trying to. And I want you to know that your feelings matter to me, even when we don't see eye to eye."

This conversation marks a turning point for Sarah and Emma. It's not a magic fix—disagreements and misunderstandings will still exist. But they've laid the foundation for better communication, one attentive listener at a time.

Expressing Needs and Boundaries: Finding Your Voice in the Family Orchestra

Inspired by Sarah's breakthrough with Emma, Mike decides to work on his communication skills, particularly when expressing his needs and setting boundaries. He realizes that his tendency to say "yes" to everyone—at work and home—has left him overwhelmed and resentful.

The perfect opportunity to practice arises when Ethan approaches him about the promised video game time.

"Dad, can we play now? You said we would!" Ethan bounces on his toes, controller in hand.

In the past, Mike might have either grudgingly agreed, despite his mountain of work, or snapped at Ethan in frustration. This time, he takes a deep breath and chooses a different approach.

"Ethan, buddy, come sit with me for a minute," Mike says, patting the couch beside him. Once Ethan is settled, Mike continues, "I know I promised we'd play, and I want you to know that spending time with you is important to me."

Ethan beams at this, but Mike holds up a hand to indicate he's not finished.

"At the same time, I have some work that I need to get done tonight. It's my responsibility, and it's important too. So, I'd like to offer you a choice."

Ethan's eyes widen with interest. He's not used to being offered choices in situations like this.

Mike lays out the options: "We can either play for 15 minutes now, and then I'll need to work for the rest of the evening, or we can wait until Saturday afternoon and have a full hour of uninterrupted game time together. Which would you prefer?"

Ethan considers this seriously. "Can I think about it?"

"Of course," Mike says, proud of his son's thoughtful response. "Take your time."

As Ethan ponders his decision, Mike marvels at how different this interaction feels. By using "I" statements to express his needs, setting clear expectations, and offering choices, he's turned a potential conflict into a collaborative problem-solving session.

After a few minutes, Ethan looks up at his dad. "I think I want to wait until Saturday," he says. "That way, we can play longer, and you won't be stressed about work."

Mike feels a surge of love for his son. "That's very considerate of you, Ethan. Thank you for understanding.

I'm looking forward to our game time on Saturday."

As Ethan scampers off, Mike realizes that by expressing his needs clearly and respectfully, he's taken care of himself and given Ethan an essential lesson in healthy communication and decision-making.

Conflict Resolution: Tuning the Family Harmony

As Sarah and Mike continue to work on their communication skills, they notice a gradual shift in the family dynamic. There's less tension, more laughter, and a growing sense of connection. But they're realistic—they know conflicts are inevitable in family life. The key is learning how to navigate these conflicts in a way that strengthens rather than damages their relationships.

One evening, an opportunity to put their new skills to the test presents itself. Emma asks to go to a Friday night party at a friend's house, but Sarah and Mike have concerns about the lack of adult supervision.

In the past, this escalated quickly into a shouting match. But this time, Sarah takes a deep breath and suggests, "Why don't we all sit down and talk about this calmly?"

The family gathers in the living room. Before they begin, Mike suggests they start with a brief prayer. "Lord," he says quietly, "please guide our discussion and help us to listen to each other with open hearts."

As they talk, each family member practices the skills they've been learning. Sarah and Mike listen actively to Emma's perspective, asking clarifying questions and acknowledging her feelings. Emma, in turn, tries to see her parents' point of view.

"I understand you want to spend time with your friends," Sarah says, "and that's important. We're just concerned about your safety."

Emma nods reluctantly. "I get that. But I feel like you don't trust me."

Instead of becoming defensive, Mike leans in. "I can see why you might feel that way. Can you help us understand what makes you feel trusted?"

As they continue to discuss, they focus on finding solutions rather than placing blame. They explore different options, considering the needs and concerns of everyone involved.

Finally, they compromise: Emma can attend the party, but Sarah will discreetly check in with the host's parents and arrange a pick-up time. Additionally, Emma agrees to text her parents hourly with updates.

"This approach seems promising," Emma remarks, her expression brightening with a hint of optimism. "I appreciate your attentiveness to my thoughts."

Sarah and Mike exchange a glance, both feeling a sense of accomplishment. They've managed to navigate a potentially explosive situation and develop a stronger family bond.

As they wrap up their discussion, Ethan asks, "Can we pray again? To say thank you?"

The family joins hands, and this time, Emma leads the prayer. "Thank you, God, for helping us talk to each other and figure things out. Please help us keep getting better at this."

In this moment, the Johnson family truly feels like a harmonious orchestra, each member playing their part to create something beautiful together.

The Ongoing Symphony of Family Communication

As the weeks pass, the Johnsons continue practicing their new communication skills. It's not always perfect—there are still moments of discord when old habits creep back in. But they're learning to recognize these moments and gently guide each other to more constructive patterns.

They've discovered that effective communication is not a destination but a journey—an ongoing process of tuning their family orchestra. Some days, they produce breathtaking harmonies. On other days, they hit a few sour notes. But through it all, they're growing closer, understanding each other better, and creating a family dynamic that resonates with love, respect, and genuine connection.

As you reflect on the Johnson family's journey, consider how you might apply these lessons to your family's communication style. Remember, every family is unique, with its challenges and strengths. The key is to keep practicing, to approach each interaction with grace and truth, and to never give up on the beautiful symphony your family can create together.

Here are some key takeaways to help you enhance your family's communication:

- Engage in attentive hearing: Deliberately strive to comprehend each household member's viewpoint. This involves eliminating diversions, sustaining visual connection, and prioritizing compassion over criticism.

- Express needs and set boundaries clearly: Use "I" statements to communicate your feelings and needs. Offer choices when appropriate, and be clear about expectations and consequences.

- Approach conflicts as opportunities for growth: When disagreements arise, start with prayer, focus on finding solutions rather than placing blame, and aim for outcomes that consider everyone's needs.

- Be patient with the process: Remember that improving family communication is an ongoing journey. Acknowledge minor achievements, gain insights from obstacles, and maintain a steady dedication to improvement.

- Model the communication style you want to see: Children often learn more from what we do than we say. You'll teach your children valuable life skills by consistently demonstrating respectful, clear, and empathetic communication.

As you move forward, remember that effective communication paves the way for establishing strong family values and rules—which will be our focus in the next chapter. By laying this open, respectful dialogue foundation, you're preparing your family to tackle more significant questions about your shared principles and how you want to live them out together.

Remember, every family has the potential to create beautiful music together. You can transform your family's communication from cacophony to symphony with patience, practice, and a commitment to grace and truth. The journey may not always be easy, but the harmony you create will be worth every effort.

75

CHAPTER FIVE

Establishing Christ-Centered Family Values

What would Jesus do if He were a stepparent today? It's an intriguing question. As you navigate the complex waters of blended family life, keeping this question in your mind can be incredibly helpful. After all, Jesus' teachings on love, compassion, and family provide a solid foundation for building strong, Christ-centered values in your home.

Let's explore the story of the Johnsons, a blended family trying to find their footing in a new life together. Their journey might inspire you to reflect on your family's values and traditions.

Mark Johnson stood in the kitchen, staring blankly at the pile of dishes in the sink. It had been another tense family dinner, with his two biological children and three stepchildren barely acknowledging each other's presence. His wife, Sarah, had retreated to the bedroom, clearly upset by the lack of unity at the table.

As he began to scrub a particularly stubborn pot, Mark wondered, "What would Jesus do in this situation?" It wasn't the first time he'd asked himself this question since marrying Sarah and blending their families six months ago, but it felt more pressing tonight than ever.

Mark and Sarah had both experienced complex divorces. They found solace in their shared faith and eventually fell in love. Their wedding day was filled with hope and joy, but merging two families with different backgrounds, traditions, and values had proven more challenging than they'd anticipated.

Mark's children, Emma (14) and Jack (10), were still grieving the loss of their nuclear family. They often acted out, pushing boundaries and testing Mark's patience. Sarah's kids - Lily (16), Max (12), and Sophie (8) - were struggling to adjust to their new living situation and Mark's presence in their lives.

Mark decided it was time for a change as he finished the dishes. He and Sarah needed to establish Christ-centered family values to unite their blended family intentionally. But where to start?

The following day, Mark shared his thoughts with Sarah over coffee. "I think we need to focus on building a strong foundation of Christian values for our family," he said. Establishing fundamental guidelines could provide direction for our interactions and decision-making processes.

Sarah nodded, her eyes lighting up with hope. "That's a great idea, Mark. But how do we do that with five kids who are all at different stages and have their ideas about family?"

Mark smiled, feeling a sense of purpose for the first time in weeks. "Well, let's start by identifying what we believe are the most important Christian values for our family. Then, we can create some new family traditions that reflect those values. And maybe we could even develop a family mission statement together."

Sarah reached across the table and squeezed his hand. "I love it. Let's give it a try."

Over the next few weeks, Mark and Sarah worked together to identify the core Christian values they wanted to instill in their blended family. They settled on three principles: love and compassion, integrity and honesty, and service and humility.

With these values in mind, they called a family meeting one Saturday afternoon. The kids slumped into the living room, eyeing each other warily and wondering what was happening.

Mark took a deep breath and began, "Kids, Sarah and I have been thinking a lot about our family lately. We know it hasn't been easy for any of you, and we want to do better. We believe that focusing on some important Christian values might help us become a stronger, more united family."

He explained the three core values they'd chosen, asking for input from each of the children. To Mark and Sarah's surprise, the kids engaged in the conversation. Emma suggested that love and compassion could mean being patient with each other as they adjusted to their new family dynamic. Max pointed out that integrity and honesty should include respecting each other's privacy and personal space.

As the discussion continued, Mark and Sarah could see a tiny spark of interest in the children's eyes. It wasn't a complete transformation, but it was a start.

Over the next few months, the Johnsons worked on incorporating these values into their daily lives. They could have been better, and there were still plenty of arguments and misunderstandings. But slowly, things began to change.

One day, Mark overheard Jack comforting Sophie after she'd had a bad day at school. "Remember what Dad and Sarah said about compassion?" Jack said. Well, this is an excellent time to practice it. Do you want to talk about what happened?"

Mark felt his heart swell with pride. It was a small moment, but it showed that their efforts were starting to pay off.

As the family became more comfortable with their core values, Mark and Sarah decided it was time to create new family traditions to reinforce these principles and help bind them together as a unit.

They started with a weekly family game night, where they could practice love and compassion by cheering each other on and being good sports. They also instituted a monthly service project, where the family would volunteer together at a local charity. This allowed them to practice humility and service while bonding over shared experiences.

One of the most meaningful traditions they started was the "Blended Family Birthday." They chose a date halfway between Mark and Sarah's wedding anniversary and celebrated it as the birthday of their blended family. Each year, they would reflect on how far they'd come, share their favorite memories from the past year, and set goals for the future.

As time passed, the Johnson family began to feel more like a cohesive unit. There were still challenges, but they had a framework for addressing issues and making decisions together.

About a year after their initial family meeting, Mark and Sarah decided it was time to create a family mission statement.

They gathered everyone in the living room again, this time with poster board and markers on the coffee table. "We've come a long way as a family," Sarah began. "Now we want to create a mission statement that reflects who we are and what we stand for."

The process could have been smoother. There were disagreements and moments of frustration. But as they worked together, something unique happened. The kids started to open up about their hopes and fears for their blended family. Lily admitted that she sometimes felt lost in the shuffle of so many siblings. Jack confessed that he worried about losing his special bond with his dad.

As they discussed these concerns, the family found ways to address them in their mission statement. After several drafts and much discussion, they finally agreed on a statement that felt right:

"The Johnson Family: Rooted in Christ's love, we strive to support and encourage each other, honor our individual histories, and grow together in faith, integrity, and service to others."

They wrote the statement on a large piece of paper and hung it prominently in their home. Mark and Sarah made a point of referring to it when making family decisions or resolving conflicts.

As the months passed, the Johnsons found that their focus on Christ-centered values and shared mission statement profoundly impacted their family dynamics. The children began to see each other as allies rather than competitors, and Mark and Sarah felt more united in their parenting approach.

Of course, it wasn't all smooth sailing. There were still arguments, misunderstandings, and moments of tension. But now they had the tools to work through these challenges together.

One evening, as Mark was tucking Sophie into bed, she asked him a question that caught him off guard. "Dad," she said (she had started calling him that a few months ago), "do you think Jesus would be proud of our family?"

Mark paused, considering her question carefully. "You know, Sophie," he replied, "I think Jesus would be proud of how hard we're trying. We're not perfect, but we're doing our best to love each other and live according to His teachings. And I believe He's with us every step of the way."

Sophie smiled and hugged him tightly. "I'm glad we're a family," she whispered.

As Mark left her room, he felt a deep sense of gratitude. The journey of blending their family had been challenging. Still, they built something beautiful and strong by focusing on Christ-centered values, creating meaningful traditions, and working together on a shared mission.

He thought back to that night in the kitchen when he had asked himself, "What would Jesus do?" While he couldn't always claim the perfect answer to that question, he knew their family was on the right path by keeping it in their minds.

As you reflect on the Johnson family's journey, consider how you might apply some of these principles to your blended family situation. Remember, every family is unique, and what works for one may not work for another. However, by prioritizing principles rooted in Christian teachings, you can establish a robust base for your non-traditional family unit.

Here are some key takeaways from the Johnsons' experience:

- Identify core Christian values that resonate with your family. For the Johnsons, it was love, compassion, integrity, honesty, service, and humility. What values are most important to your family?

- Create new family traditions that reinforce your chosen values and help bind your blended family together. This could be anything from a weekly game night to an annual "Blended Family Birthday" celebration.

- Develop a family mission statement that involves input from all family members. This process can help everyone feel heard and invested in the family's direction.

- Use your family's values and mission statement to guide conflict resolution decisions. This provides a consistent framework for addressing challenges.

- Be patient and persistent. Building a strong, Christ-centered blended family takes time and effort. Celebrate small victories and learn from setbacks.

Remember, just as the Johnsons discovered, establishing Christ-centered family values in a blended family is an ongoing process. Success demands forbearance, empathy, and flexibility. But with faith as your foundation and love as your guide, you can create a harmonious and joy-filled home that honors God and nurtures each family member.

As you move forward, ask yourself, "What would Jesus do?" Let His teachings on love, forgiveness, and family guide your actions and decisions. And remember, just as Jesus welcomed all into His family, you can create a blended family that reflects His inclusive love.

In the next chapter, we'll build on this foundation of values as we tackle the practical aspects of discipline in a blended family. But for now, take some time to reflect on your family's values and consider how you might start implementing some of these ideas in your own home.

May God bless and guide you as you continue this blended family journey rooted in His love and wisdom.

CHAPTER SIX

Disciplining with Love and Wisdom

Those who refrain from correcting their offspring demonstrate a lack of proper care, while parents who genuinely love their children provide measured guidance and correction.

You take a deep breath, steeling yourself for what's sure to be another challenging evening. You can hear the raised voices inside the house as you pull into the driveway. Your stepson, Jake, is at it again.

At 13, Jake's rebellious streak has been growing stronger by the day. You've only been married to his father, Tom, for eight months, but it feels like you've aged years in that time. The constant battles over homework and chores and Jake's increasingly defiant attitude have left you exhausted and questioning whether you're cut out for this stepparenting gig.

As you walk through the front door, you're greeted by the all-too-familiar sight of Tom and Jake locked in a heated argument. Jake's face is flushed with anger, his fists clenched at his sides. Tom looks equally frustrated, his voice rising as he threatens to ground Jake for a month if he doesn't shape up.

You hang back, unsure of your place in this family drama. Should you jump in and try to mediate? Should you stay out of it entirely? Your uncertainty is palpable, mirroring many stepparents' confusion about discipline in blended families.

As the shouting match continues, your mind drifts back to your conversation with your small group leader at church last week. Sarah, a seasoned stepmother herself, had shared some wisdom that now seems particularly relevant.

"Remember," Sarah had said, her eyes severe but kind, "discipline isn't about punishment. It's about teaching, guiding, and ultimately, showing love. When we discipline with wisdom and compassion, we're helping shape our children's character and preparing them for life."

You nodded, thinking it sounded good in theory but wondering how to implement it in your complicated family situation. As you watch Tom and Jake's argument spiral further out of control, you realize it's time to try a different approach.

Taking another deep breath, you step forward. "Hey guys,"

you say, keeping your voice calm and steady. "Why don't we all take a few minutes to cool down? Then maybe we can talk about what's going on here."

Tom and Jake both turn to look at you, surprise evident on their faces. They'd been so caught up in their argument that they'd forgotten you were even there. After a moment's hesitation, Tom nods and steps back. Jake, still scowling, stomps off to his room and slams the door.

You turn to Tom, placing a gentle hand on his arm. "What happened?" you ask softly.

Tom sighs, running a hand through his hair. "I found out Jake's been lying about doing his homework. His teacher called today – apparently, he hasn't turned in an assignment in weeks. When I confronted him about it, he just exploded."

You nod, understanding dawning. Jake's behavior has been deteriorating for a while now, but this feels like a new low. As you and Tom discuss the situation, you can't help but think back to Sarah's words about discipline and love.

"Maybe," you suggest hesitantly, "we need to approach this differently. Instead of punishing Jake, what if we try to figure out why he's acting this way?"

Tom looks skeptical, but he's willing to listen. You can see hope in his eyes as you share some of the ideas you've been mulling over since your talk with Sarah. Together, you start to formulate a plan.

An hour later, you gently knock on Jake's door. "Can we come in?" you ask. There's a muffled grunt from inside, which you take as permission. You and Tom enter the room, finding Jake sprawled on his bed, headphones on, and a scowl still etched on his face.

Instead of launching into a lecture, you sit down on the edge of the bed. Tom pulls up Jake's desk chair, his posture open and non-threatening. "We'd like to talk," Tom says, his voice calm. "But more importantly, we'd like to listen. Can you tell us what's been going on?"

Jake looks surprised, then suspicious. But as you and Tom maintain your calm, open demeanor, he slowly opens up. There's a lot more going on than just missed homework assignments. Jake's been struggling to adjust to his new school, overwhelmed by the increased workload and social pressures. He's also been missing his mom, who moved out of state for a new job six months ago.

As Jake talks, you and Tom listen without judgment. You ask

questions to understand better, showing genuine interest in Jake's feelings and experiences. By the end of the conversation, Jake's defiant attitude has softened, replaced by a look of relief at finally being heard.

Now comes the tricky part – addressing Jake's behavior while showing love and support. You and Tom exchange glances, silently agreeing to implement your new approach.

"Jake," Tom begins, "we hear you and understand things have been tough. But lying about homework and falling behind in school isn't the answer. We need to figure out how to get you back on track."

Jake tenses, clearly expecting a harsh punishment. But instead, Tom continues, "We're going to work on this together. First, let's set up a daily homework check-in. You'll show me your assignments daily, and we'll help you stay organized. We'll also contact your teachers to see if you can get extra help or extended deadlines to catch up."

You chime in, "And Jake, we know you're missing your mom. What if we set up a regular video call schedule with her? Maybe every Sunday evening? We can also look into some activities or clubs at school that might help you meet new friends."

Jake looks stunned. "You're... not grounding me?" he asks hesitantly.

Tom shakes his head. "No, not this time. But Jake, this is your chance to turn things around. We're here to support you, but you must also put in the effort. If we don't see improvement or the lying continues, we must consider stricter consequences. Does that sound fair?"

Jake nods slowly, a mix of relief and determination crossing his face. "Yeah... I think I can do that."

As you leave Jake's room that night, you feel a glimmer of hope. It's just a start, but feels like a step in the right direction. Over the next few weeks, you and Tom will work to implement your new approach to discipline, keeping in mind the biblical principles of consistency, fairness, and balancing correction with affirmation.

It can be challenging. There are still arguments and moments of frustration. But gradually, you start to see positive changes. Jake becomes more open with you and Tom, seeking help with his homework instead of hiding his struggles. His grades begin to improve, and the defiant outbursts become less frequent.

One evening, about a month after your heart-to-heart with Jake, you're all sitting around the dinner table when Jake clears his throat nervously. "I, uh, I got my math test back today," he says, not quite meeting your eyes.

You and Tom exchange a worried glance. Math has been Jake's most challenging subject. "And?" Tom prompts gently.

A slow smile spreads across Jake's face as he pulls a crumpled paper from his backpack. "I got a B+!" he announces proudly.

The table erupts in cheers and congratulations. As you watch Tom pull Jake into a bear hug, warmth spreads through your chest. This is what discipline with love looks like, you realize. It's not about punishment or control but guiding, supporting, and celebrating growth.

Later that night, as you're getting ready for bed, Tom wraps his arms around you from behind. "Thank you," he murmurs into your hair.

"For what?" you ask, leaning back into his embrace.

"For helping me see a different way to handle things with Jake. Thank you for being patient with us as we figure this out. For loving us, even when we're not very lovable."

You turn in his arms, meeting his gaze. "That's what family is all about," you say softly. "We're in this together."

As you drift off to sleep that night, you reflect on how far you've come in your stepparenting journey. There's still a long road ahead, but you feel more equipped to handle the challenges now. You've learned that effective discipline in a blended family requires wisdom, patience, and love.

Your mind wanders back to the biblical proverb that started this chapter: Those who avoid correcting their children's behavior lack genuine care. At the same time, parents who genuinely love their offspring provide thoughtful guidance and appropriate discipline. You now understand that the "rod" isn't about physical punishment but guidance, correction, and teaching. It's about setting boundaries with love, being consistent in your approach, and always keeping the child's best interests at heart.

In the following weeks and months, you continue refining your approach to discipline in your blended family. You learn to support Tom's role as the primary disciplinarian while gradually increasing your involvement as Jake becomes more comfortable with your place in the family. You discover the power of positive reinforcement, celebrating small victories and encouraging good behavior rather than just focusing on correcting the bad.

Of course, there are still challenges. Jake has his moody teenage moments, and there are times when you and Tom disagree on the best course of action. But you've learned to approach these moments gracefully, always returning to the foundational principles of love, consistency, and mutual respect.

As you navigate this complex terrain of stepfamily discipline, you keep a few key points in mind:

- Discipline is about teaching, not punishing. Your goal is to guide Jake towards making better choices, not to make him suffer for his mistakes.

- Consistency is crucial. You and Tom work to present a united front, agreeing on rules and consequences beforehand and sticking to them.

- Positive reinforcement is powerful. You make a conscious effort to praise Jake's efforts and improvements, no matter how small.

- Respect boundaries. As a stepparent, you recognize that your role in discipline may differ from Tom's, and you're careful to respect Jake's feelings as he adjusts to your presence.

- Clear exchanges of information are crucial. You keep active dialogue channels with Jake, Tom, and Jake's mother, ensuring all parties understand and agree on rules and outcomes.

One sunny Saturday afternoon, as you're cheering Jake on at his soccer game, you have a moment of clarity. Watching him sprint down the field, determination etched on his face, you realize how much he's grown – not just physically but emotionally and maturity-wise – in the past few months.

You think back to that night of the big homework blow-up and how hopeless and frustrated you'd felt. If someone had told you then that you'd be here now, feeling proud and connected to your stepson, you might not have believed them.

But here you are, part of a family learning to blend, grow, and love each other through the tough times. As Jake scores a goal and turns to the sidelines with a huge grin, searching for you and Tom in the crowd, you feel a surge of love and pride.

You think this is what it's all about. This is why we put in discipline, set boundaries, and have tough conversations. It's all so we can have moments like these—joy, connection, and family.

As you and Tom envelop Jake in a group hug after the game, his sweaty, grinning face pressed between you, you silently thank God for the wisdom and patience He's granted you on this journey. You know there will be more challenges ahead – Jake is, after all, only 13, with all the turbulence of the teenage years still to come. But you feel ready to face whatever comes, armed with love, wisdom, and the support of your blended family.

That evening, as you're all lounging in the living room, Jake is playing a video game while you and Tom read; Jake suddenly pauses his game and turns to you both. "Hey," he says, a bit shyly. "I just wanted to say... thanks. For, you know, not giving up on me. For helping me do better."

You feel tears prick at your eyes as Tom affectionately reaches out to ruffle Jake's hair. "We're a family, buddy," Tom says. We're in this together."

Jake nods, then turns to you specifically. "Thanks for being patient with me. I know I wasn't always nice when you first came, but... I'm glad you're here."

You swallow past the lump in your throat, touched beyond words. "I'm glad I'm here too, Jake," you manage to say.

As Jake turns back to his game, you catch Tom's eye. The love and gratitude you see there mirror your feelings. You've been working towards this – a family united by love, respect, and, yes, wise and loving discipline.

You know the journey isn't over. There will be more challenges and more moments of frustration and doubt. But you also know you have the tools to face those challenges now. You understand the delicate balance required in stepfamily discipline, the need for consistency, fairness, and always, always love.

You feel a deep sense of peace as you snuggle closer to Tom on the couch, watching Jake navigate his virtual world with the determination he's shown to improve his real-life behavior. You're not just Jake's stepmother anymore – you're a vital part of this family, helping to guide, support, and love this wonderful, complex boy as he grows into adulthood.

And really, isn't that what parenting – step or otherwise – is all about? Guiding with love, disciplining with wisdom, and always pointing towards growth and healing. As you drift off to sleep that night, you offer a prayer of thanks for the lessons you've learned and the love surrounding you in this beautiful, blended family of yours.

CHAPTER SEVEN

Healing From Grief and Loss

Did you know that over 60% of blended families report

struggling with unresolved grief issues even years after their formation? It's a startling statistic but likely won't surprise you if you navigate your blended family journey. Grief and loss are often unexpected companions as you work to build your new family unit, but understanding and addressing these emotions is crucial for creating a solid foundation.

Let's dive into Sarah's story to explore how grief can manifest in blended families and discover strategies for healing:

You first met Sarah at a local support group for blended families. Her warm smile didn't quite reach her eyes as she introduced herself, explaining that she and her new husband, Mark, had been struggling to merge their families for the past year. Sarah had two children from her previous marriage – Ethan (10) and Lily (8) – while Mark brought his daughter, Zoe (12), into their new home.

"I thought I was prepared," Sarah confided during a coffee meetup after group. "I'd done all this reading about blended families, made lists of potential issues, even had the kids in therapy before the wedding. But no one warned me about the grief."

You nodded encouragingly, sensing Sarah needed to unburden herself.

"It's not just one thing," she continued. "It's this constant ache like something's missing. And then I feel guilty for feeling that way because I love Mark, and I'm happy we're together. But sometimes I look around the dinner table, and it feels... wrong. Does that make any sense?"

It made perfect sense. Sarah was grappling with one of the most common, yet least discussed, challenges of blended family life: the loss of the "ideal" family.

Recognizing Different Types of Loss

As Sarah shared more of her story, it became clear she was dealing with multiple layers of grief:

1. Loss of the "Ideal" Family: Like many people, Sarah had grown up with a specific vision of what her family would look like. Even though her first marriage had ended, part of her still mourned the loss of that dream. While filled with love, the reality of her blended family didn't match the picture she'd held in her mind for so long.

2. Loss of Exclusive Parent-Child Relationships: Sarah struggled with jealousy when she saw Zoe and Mark's close bond. She also felt guilty for resenting Mark's time with her children, even though she logically knew it was vital for them to build relationships.

3. Loss of Familiar Routines and Traditions: The family pizza and movie night that had been a staple in Sarah's household every Friday now felt awkward with Zoe's preference for different foods and Mark's work schedule. Holiday celebrations became a minefield of competing traditions and loyalties.

As you listened to Sarah, you recognized the weight of these losses. They might seem small individually, but collectively, they created a significant emotional burden. You gently pointed out to Sarah that what she felt was a normal part of the blended family adjustment process.

"Really?" Sarah asked, a glimmer of hope in her eyes. "Sometimes I feel like I'm the only one struggling with this. Mark seems so... fine with everything."

You assured Sarah that it was common for family members to process these changes at different rates. You also emphasized the importance of open communication about these feelings, even (and especially) when they're uncomfortable.

Guiding Children Through Grief

As your conversation with Sarah continued, she revealed another layer of concern: her children's emotional well-being.

"Ethan's been acting out at school," Sarah confided. "And Lily barely speaks anymore. I know they're hurting, but I don't know how to help them when I struggle."

You nodded sympathetically, recognizing the challenge of guiding children through grief while navigating your own emotions. You shared some strategies that have helped other blended families:

1. Validating Emotions: Encourage Sarah to create a safe space where all family members can express their feelings without judgment. This might involve regular family meetings or one-on-one time with each child.

2. Creating Space for Expression: Suggest alternative ways for the children to process their emotions, such as through art, journaling, or physical activities. Sometimes, kids (and adults) need non-verbal outlets for their grief.

3. Seeking Specialized Support: Reassure Sarah that consulting a skilled expert, like a counselor or consultant well-versed in intricate family dynamics, is appropriate and potentially beneficial.

You also shared a story from your own experience, recalling a tough day when your stepson had an emotional outburst during what was supposed to be a fun family outing.

"In that moment, I realized he wasn't just being difficult," you explained. "He was grieving the loss of his 'old' family, even though he cared about all of us. Once I understood that, responding with empathy instead of frustration became easier."

Sarah nodded, a look of recognition crossing her face. "I never thought about it that way," she mused. "I've been so focused on making everything 'work' that I forgot to just... let us all feel what we're feeling."

Finding Healing Through Faith

As your conversation with Sarah drew close, she hesitantly brought up another aspect of her struggle. "I feel like I should be handling this better," she admitted. "We're a Christian family, and I know God has a plan for us. But sometimes it's hard to see it."

Your expression brightened supportively as you saw a chance to explore the role of spiritual beliefs in fostering recovery and growth. You shared your experience of finding comfort and strength in your beliefs during difficult times in your blended family journey.

"For me," you explained, "turning to my faith helped me reframe our challenges as opportunities for growth. It wasn't always easy, but focusing on God's love and guidance gave me the strength to keep moving forward."

You went on to discuss some specific ways that Sarah and her family might incorporate their faith into their healing process:

1. Embracing God's Comfort: Encourage Sarah to use her faith for solace during challenging moments. This might involve prayer, meditation on specific Bible verses, or seeking support from her church community.

2. Practicing Forgiveness: Remind Sarah that forgiveness – of herself, her ex-spouse, and other family members – is a crucial part of the healing process. While it's not always easy, approaching forgiveness as an act of faith can be powerful.

3. Reframing Loss as Opportunity: Help Sarah see how their family's challenges can be opportunities to grow closer to God and each other. This might involve looking for "blessings in disguise" or focusing on how overcoming difficulties together can strengthen their family bond.

As you wrapped up your conversation, Sarah seemed lighter more hopeful. "Thank you," she said earnestly. "I feel like I have a roadmap or a starting point. It won't be easy, but it helps to know we're not alone."

You squeezed her hand reassuringly. "You're not alone," you affirmed. "And remember, healing is a process. Be patient with yourself and your family as you navigate this journey together."

You continued to check in with Sarah in the following weeks and months. There were ups and downs, as there always are in blended family life, but you noticed a gradual shift in her perspective. She seemed more at peace, better equipped to handle the challenges that arose.

One day, several months after your initial conversation, Sarah shared a breakthrough moment:

"We were having dinner last night," she recounted, her eyes shining. It was nothing special, just a regular Tuesday. But I looked around the table—at Mark helping Lily with her homework, Zoe and Ethan arguing good-naturedly over the last dinner roll—and I felt this wave of... contentment, I guess? It wasn't perfect, but it was ours. And for the first time, that felt like enough."

Sarah's journey illustrates a fundamental truth about healing from grief and loss in blended families: it's not about erasing the past or pretending that everything is perfect. Instead, it's about acknowledging the losses, working through the pain, and gradually building a new sense of family that honors both the past and the present.

As you reflect on Sarah's story and your own experiences, consider these critical takeaways for healing from grief and loss in blended families:

- Recognize that grief is an ordinary and necessary part of the blended family journey. Give yourself and your family members permission to feel and express their emotions.

- Create safe spaces for all family members to share their feelings through regular family meetings, one-on-one time, or alternative forms of expression like art or physical activities.

- Don't hesitate to seek professional help if you or your family are struggling. A therapist experienced in blended family dynamics can provide valuable guidance and support.

- Draw upon your spiritual beliefs for solace and resilience. Use practices such as prayer, contemplation, and support from your faith community to aid in your recovery process.

- Practice forgiveness – of yourself and others – as an

ongoing process. Forgiveness doesn't mean forgetting or excusing past hurts but freeing yourself from resentment.

- Look for opportunities for growth and connection amidst the challenges. Try to reframe difficulties as chances to strengthen your family bond and deepen your faith.

Remember, healing from grief and loss in a blended family is rarely a linear process. There will likely be setbacks and difficult days even as you make progress. The key is approaching the journey with patience, compassion, and a willingness to keep moving forward, one step at a time.

As you continue to work through your grief and help your family members do the same, you'll likely find that the process creates a more robust, more resilient family unit. The shared experience of acknowledging losses, supporting each other through difficult emotions, and finding new ways to connect can create a unique and powerful bond.

It's also important to celebrate the small victories along the way. Did you have a breakthrough conversation with your stepchild? Did you manage to navigate a potentially contentious holiday without significant conflict? Did you find a new tradition that everyone enjoys? Take time to acknowledge and appreciate these moments of progress.

As your family heals and grows more robust, you'll be better equipped to tackle other challenges that arise. This brings us to our next chapter, where we'll explore strategies for building a positive co-parenting relationship—an essential skill for long-term blended family harmony.

But before we move on, take a moment to reflect on your blended family journey. Where have you experienced loss? How have you and your family members expressed grief? What strategies have you found helpful in the healing process?

Remember, every blended family's path is unique, but you're not walking it alone. By sharing our stories, struggles, and successes, we can support and learn from each other, creating a community of understanding and hope for all blended families.

As you close this chapter and prepare to delve into the world of co-parenting, carry with you the knowledge that healing is possible. The grief and loss you've experienced are authentic and valid, but they don't define your family's future. Through perseverance, empathy, and openness to the difficulties and rewards of non-traditional family dynamics, you create a basis for a fulfilling and significant household experience.

Take a deep breath, credit yourself for your work so far, and get ready to explore the next phase of your blended family journey. Remember, every step forward, no matter how small, is progress. You've got this!

CHAPTER EIGHT

Navigating Co-Parenting Relationships

How you handle your co-parenting relationship can profoundly shape your children's emotional well-being and future relationships. When parents work together, despite their differences, children thrive.

Imagine this: It's a crisp autumn Saturday morning, and

you're sitting at your kitchen table, sipping coffee and scrolling through your phone. Your 10-year-old daughter, Sophia, bounds into the room, her eyes excitedly shining.

"Mom! Dad just texted me. He said he could take me to the fall festival today! Can I go? Please?"

You feel a knot forming in your stomach. This is the first you've heard about the festival, and you had plans to take Sophia shopping for new winter boots this afternoon. You take a deep breath, reminding yourself that your reaction matters more than you might realize.

"That sounds like fun, sweetie," you say, smiling. "Let me text your dad quickly to sort out the details, okay?"

As you reach for your phone, you're transported back to when communicating with your ex-husband, Mark, was anything but cordial. The first year after your divorce was a minefield of hurt feelings, miscommunication, and power struggles. Every interaction felt like a battle, with Sophia caught in the crossfire.

But then, something changed. You both realized that your constant conflict was taking a toll on Sophia. She'd become withdrawn, her grades were slipping, and her ordinarily bubbly personality had dimmed. It was a wake-up call that forced you and Mark to reevaluate your approach to co-parenting.

As you type out a message to Mark, you're grateful for how far you've come. Your thumb hovers over the send button as you reread your text:

"Hey Mark, Sophia just told me about the fall festival. Sounds fun! I had planned to take her boot shopping this afternoon. Let's work out a schedule so she can do both. Let me know what you think."

You hit send and turn back to Sophia, who vibrates with anticipation. "Alright, kiddo. Let's see what your dad says, and we'll figure out a plan, okay?"

Sophia nods, her smile brightening the entire kitchen. As you wait for Mark's response, you reflect on the journey that brought you to this point of relatively smooth co-parenting. It wasn't easy, but the peace for your family has been worth every problematic conversation and compromise.

Your phone buzzes with Mark's reply: "Thanks for letting me know. How about I pick her up at 11 for the festival, and you can take her shopping after I drop her off at 4? That work for you?"

You smile, remembering when such a simple exchange would have been unthinkable. "That sounds perfect," you reply. Have fun, you two!"

As you share the plan with an ecstatic Sophia, you can't help but feel proud of how far you and Mark have come in your co-parenting journey. It's a stark contrast to where you started, and the positive impact on Sophia is undeniable.

Let's rewind and explore how you and Mark navigated the choppy waters of co-parenting to reach this point of collaboration and mutual respect.

Establishing Boundaries with Ex-Partners

In the early days after your divorce, boundaries were practically non-existent between you and Mark. Every interaction seemed to devolve into rehashing old arguments or making passive-aggressive comments about each other's parenting styles. It was exhausting, and worse, it was hurting Sophia.

The turning point came during a parent-teacher conference at Sophia's school. As you and Mark sat across from Mrs. Thompson, Sophia's fourth-grade teacher, the tension between you was palpable. Mrs. Thompson cleared her throat nervously before speaking.

"I've noticed that Sophia seems... distracted lately," she

began. "Her grades have slipped, and she has trouble focusing in class. Is everything okay at home?"

You and Mark exchanged guilty glances. It was a wake-up call you both needed.

That evening, after Sophia had gone to bed, you called Mark. "We need to talk," you said, your voice steady despite your nerves. "About Sophia, about us, about how we're handling this co-parenting thing."

To your surprise, Mark agreed without hesitation. "You're right," he said, sounding as tired as you felt. "This isn't working, and Sophia's paying the price."

Over the next few weeks, you and Mark had several difficult but necessary conversations. You both realized you needed to establish clear boundaries to be effective co-parents. Here's what you agreed on:

1. Focus on Sophia's needs: Every decision, every conversation, and every interaction would be centered on what was best for Sophia. Your grievances with each other would take a backseat to her well-being.

2. Limit discussions to parenting matters: You agreed to focus solely on Sophia and co-parenting issues. No more

rehashing the past or discussing personal lives unless it directly affected Sophia.

3. Respect privacy and new relationships: You both acknowledged that you were entitled to move on with your lives. You agreed not to pry into each other's personal affairs or speak negatively about new partners before Sophia.

These boundaries didn't magically solve all your problems overnight but provided a framework for healthier interactions. Over time, as you both consistently respected these boundaries, the tension between you began to ease.

Remember the first time you put these boundaries into practice? It was during Sophia's spring piano recital. As you sat in the audience, waiting for Sophia's turn to perform, you felt Mark slide into the seat next to you.

"Hey," he whispered. "How's she doing? Is she nervous?"

For a moment, you were tempted to make a snarky comment about how he would know if he'd been to more of her practices. But you caught yourself, remembering your agreement to focus on Sophia's needs.

"A little nervous," you replied instead. "But she's been

practicing hard. I think she'll do great."

Mark nodded, and you both turned your attention to the stage. As Sophia walked out, her little face was a mix of excitement and terror, and you felt Mark's hand squeeze your arm.

"We did that," he whispered, his voice full of pride. "That's our girl."

In that moment, you realized that your new boundaries weren't just about avoiding conflict. They were about creating a space where you could be Sophia's parents together but separately. It was the first time since the divorce that you felt like a team again.

Collaborative Decision-Making

With your new boundaries in place, you and Mark were ready to tackle the following challenge: making decisions together for Sophia's benefit. This proved trickier than anticipated, as you both had different parenting styles and priorities.

The first major test came when it was time to decide on Sophia's summer activities. You wanted her to attend an academic enrichment camp to boost her confidence in math and science while Mark was pushing for a sports camp to help her stay active and make new friends.

Previously, such a dispute could have escalated into an intense conflict, with each of you stubbornly maintaining your position and rejecting any middle ground. However, equipped with recently acquired strategies for collaborative parenting, you tackled the issue novelly.

You suggested a video call to discuss the summer plans. As you logged on, you reminded yourself to keep an open mind and focus on Sophia's best interests.

"So, about this summer camp situation," you began, "I know we have different ideas, but let's figure out what would be best for Sophia."

Mark nodded; his expression was severe but open. "Agreed. Why don't you tell me why the academic camp is important?"

You explained your concerns about Sophia's recent struggles in math and how you thought the camp might help boost her confidence. Mark listened attentively and asked questions to understand your perspective better.

When it was his turn, Mark shared his worries about Sophia becoming too passive and missing out on social opportunities during the summer. You nodded along, seeing the validity in his points.

As you discussed, an idea began to form. "What if," you suggested, "we split the summer? She could do the academic camp for the first three weeks and then the sports camp for the last three?"

Mark's face lit up. "That's... a great idea. We could even see if she could do any weekend sports programs during the academic camp weeks to keep her active."

By the end of the call, you had a comprehensive summer plan that addressed your concerns and, most importantly, seemed like something Sophia would enjoy. It was a breakthrough moment in your co-parenting relationship.

This experience taught you both valuable lessons about collaborative decision-making:

1. Share important information: You both realized the importance of informing each other about Sophia's progress, challenges, and needs in various areas of her life.

2. Coordinate rules and expectations: To stabilize Sophia, you agreed to maintain consistent rules and expectations across both households.

3. Plan for special events and holidays: You started using a

shared online calendar to coordinate schedules, including holidays, school events, and extracurricular activities.

These strategies helped you and Mark navigate increasingly complex decisions as Sophia grew older. From choosing electives in middle school to discussing curfews and dating rules in her teen years, you found yourselves working together more smoothly than you ever thought possible.

Managing Conflict with Ex-Partners

Despite your best efforts, conflicts still arose from time to time. The key was learning how to manage these disagreements to minimize their impact on Sophia and your co-parenting relationship.

One particularly challenging situation occurred when Sophia was 13. She came home from a weekend at Mark's house with a new smartphone – something you had both agreed she wasn't ready for yet.

Your initial reaction was fury. How dare Mark go behind your back and undermine your joint decision? You were tempted to call him immediately and give him a piece of your mind. But as your finger hovered over his name in your contacts, you remembered the progress you'd made and the impact your actions would have on Sophia.

Instead of making that angry call, you took a deep breath and texted: "Hey Mark, can we talk about Sophia's new phone when you have a moment? I thought we had agreed to wait on that."

Mark responded quickly: "Sorry, I should have discussed it with you first. Can we video chat after Sophia goes to bed?"

That evening, as you logged into the video call, you were

determined to keep calm and focus on finding a solution. Mark looked apologetic as his face appeared on the screen.

"I'm sorry," he began. "I know we had agreed to wait, but Sophia made some compelling arguments, and I guess I got caught up in the moment."

You took a deep breath before responding. "I understand, but we must present a united front on big decisions like this. Can you walk me through your thinking?"

As Mark explained his reasons for giving Sophia the phone – concerns about her safety when she started taking the bus to school, wanting her to be able to contact either of you quickly – you found yourself nodding along. These were valid points you hadn't considered before.

"Okay," you said when he finished. "I see where you're coming from. But I'm still worried about social media access and screen time. How about we collaborate to set up some guidelines and parental controls?"

Mark agreed readily, and you spent the next hour researching and discussing various options. By the end of the call, you had a comprehensive plan for managing Sophia's phone use that you both felt comfortable with.

This experience reinforced several critical strategies for managing conflict in your co-parenting relationship:

1. Practice self-control. By calming down before reacting, you avoid escalating the situation and can approach the problem more rationally.

2. Use neutral communication methods: Text and video chat allow you time to collect your thoughts and communicate more effectively.

3. Seek common ground: By listening to Mark's perspective and finding areas of agreement, you were able to work together to find a solution.

4. Focus on solutions, not blame: Instead of dwelling on Mark's breach of your agreement, you channeled your energy into creating a plan for the future.

As the years went by, you and Mark became more adept at handling conflicts when they arose. You learned to anticipate and discuss potential issues proactively, often heading off problems before they could develop.

The Impact of Healthy Co-Parenting

As you watch Sophia climb into Mark's car for their day at the fall festival, you can't help but marvel at how far you've all come. The smiling, confident teenager waving goodbye bears little resemblance to the withdrawn, struggling child from those early post-divorce days.

Your phone buzzes with a text from Mark: "She's already planning our whole day. Thanks for being flexible with the schedule. Do you want me to pick up dinner for her on the way back?"

You smile as you type your reply: "Sounds great. Have fun, you two!"

As you close the front door and head inside to prepare for your afternoon shopping trip, you reflect on the journey of the past few years. It hasn't always been easy, but Sophia's happiness and well-being clearly show the rewards of your efforts.

Here are the key takeaways from your co-parenting journey:

- Establish clear boundaries: Focus on your child's needs, limit discussions to parenting matters, and respect each other's privacy and new relationships.

- Practice collaborative decision-making: Share important information, coordinate rules and expectations across households, and plan for special events and holidays together.

- Manage conflicts constructively: Exercise self-control, use neutral communication methods, and seek solutions rather than assigning blame.

- Stay committed to the process. Healthy co-parenting is an ongoing journey that requires consistent effort and adaptability.

- Focus on the positive impact: Your efforts to maintain a healthy co-parenting relationship profoundly affect your child's emotional well-being and future relationships.

As you navigate your co-parenting journey, remember that progress often comes in small steps. Each positive interaction, each conflict resolved peacefully, and each decision made collaboratively contributes to a healthier family dynamic. It's not about being perfect; it's about consistently striving to put your child's needs first and working together to create a nurturing environment across both households.

Your story doesn't end here. As Sophia grows and faces new challenges, you and Mark will continue to adapt your co-parenting strategies. But with the foundation you've built – of respect, communication, and collaboration – you're well-equipped to face whatever comes your way.

As you go about your day, take a moment to appreciate how far you've come in your co-parenting journey. And remember, every time you choose cooperation over conflict and put Sophia's needs first, you're not just making her life better – you're teaching her valuable lessons about relationships, resilience, and love that will serve her well throughout her life.

As you prepare for your shopping trip with Sophia later, you look forward to hearing about her day at the festival. And you realize, with a sense of quiet pride, that this is what successful co-parenting looks like: two parents working together, creating a tapestry of love and support for their child, even when they're no longer together.

CHAPTER NINE

Stewarding Family Resources

As you settle into your favorite chair with a steaming cup of coffee in hand, you can't help but feel a mix of excitement and apprehension. Today's the day you and your spouse have set aside to tackle your blended family's finances. The task seems daunting, but you know it's necessary. As you wait for your partner to join you, your mind wanders to a familiar story – the Parable of the Talents.

You recall how the master in the parable entrusted his servants with different amounts of money. Some invested wisely and multiplied their resources, while one buried his talent out of fear. It strikes you that managing your family's finances is similar. You have resources entrusted to you, and it's your responsibility to steward them wisely for the benefit of your blended family.

Your spouse enters the room, laptop in hand, ready to dive into the numbers. As you begin your financial planning session, you can't help but think about how this process mirrors the lessons from that ancient parable.

"Ready to tackle this?" your spouse asks, a mixture of

determination and nervousness in their voice.

You nod, taking a deep breath. "Let's do it. I was thinking about the Parable of the Talents. We're like those servants tasked with managing what we've been given."

Your spouse smiles, catching onto your train of thought. "That's an interesting way to look at it. So, will we bury our talents in the backyard or try to multiply them?"

You chuckle, "Definitely multiply. But let's start by taking stock of what we have and where we want to go."

As you begin to discuss your financial situation, you realize that managing money in a blended family comes with unique challenges. There's child support to consider, different spending habits to reconcile, and the delicate balance of providing for biological and stepchildren equally.

"You know," you muse, "I think there are some key principles we can apply here, just like in the parable. Let's start with generosity and contentment."

Your spouse nods thoughtfully. "That's a good point. Getting caught up in wanting more is easy, especially when we're now trying to provide for a larger family. But being content with what we have and still finding ways to be generous – that's important."

You think about how this principle could play out in your daily lives. It could mean being satisfied with your current home instead of stretching your budget for a bigger one. Or it's about finding ways to give to causes you care about, even if the amounts are small.

"Exactly," you agree. "And I think the next principle we must focus on is wise planning and budgeting. We can't multiply our resources if we don't know where they're going in the first place."

Your spouse opens a spreadsheet on the laptop. "I've started tracking our expenses here. It's a bit eye-opening to see where our money goes each month."

As you pour over the numbers together, you realize how crucial open communication about money is in your blended family. You discuss your different approaches to spending and saving, working to find common ground and shared goals.

"I never realized how differently we viewed certain expenses," your spouse admits. "This conversation is constructive."

You nod in agreement. "It's not always easy to talk about money, but it's important, especially in our situation. We need to be on the same page to make this work."

As you continue your financial planning session, you tackle more complex situations unique to blended families. Child support payments come up, and you both acknowledge their emotional and economic impact.

"It's a balancing act," you sigh. "We need to fulfill our obligations to the kids from previous marriages while also ensuring we're providing equally for our family now."

Your spouse reaches out and squeezes your hand. "It is tough, but we're in this together. Let's look at our budget and see where we can adjust to make it work for everyone."

The conversation shifts to inheritance and estate planning – another sensitive topic in blended families. You discuss the importance of having clear plans in place to avoid potential conflicts down the line.

Your spouse suggests we consult with a lawyer specializing in blended family estate planning. It's essential to protect everyone's interests and make our wishes clear.

You agree, making a note to schedule an appointment. As you work through these complex financial situations, you're reminded of the servants in the parable who invested their talents wisely. It takes effort and sometimes professional help, but you're committed to managing your family's resources responsibly.

As your planning session continues, your thoughts turn to the children. "You know," you say, "One of the most important things we can do is teach our kids about financial stewardship. If we're going to manage our resources wisely, we need to pass those skills on to them, too."

Your spouse nods enthusiastically. "Absolutely. But how do we do that in a way that's appropriate for all their different ages?"

You brainstorm together, coming up with ideas for age-appropriate money lessons. For the younger kids, you decide to start with basic concepts like saving and spending using clear jars or piggy banks. For the older ones, you discuss introducing more complex ideas like budgeting and investing.

"And we can't forget about modeling responsible spending and saving," you add. "They're watching us, after all."

Your spouse laughs, "Oh, I know. Remember when little Sarah repeated my comment about the shoes being 'too expensive' in the store? Kids pick up on everything."

You agree to be more mindful of how you talk about and handle money in front of the children. You also discuss ways to encourage charitable giving, such as instilling a sense of generosity in your kids from an early age.

"What if we set aside a portion of their allowance for giving?" your spouse suggests. "We could let them choose a cause they care about and donate regularly."

You love the idea, seeing it as a practical way to teach the kids about the joy of generosity.

As your planning session winds down, you feel a sense of accomplishment. You've tackled some tough topics, made important decisions, and set goals for your family's financial future. It hasn't been easy, but you know it's worth the effort.

"You know," you say, leaning back in your chair, "I think we've done pretty well with our 'talents' today. We're not burying them in the backyard, that's for sure."

Your spouse smiles, closing the laptop. "Not. We're investing them in our family and future and teaching our kids valuable lessons. I'd say the master would be pleased."

As you clean up from your planning session, you reflect on the journey ahead. Managing finances in a blended family is an ongoing process, not a one-time event. It will take continued effort, open communication, and a commitment to wise stewardship. But you're ready for the challenge; knowing the principles you've discussed today will guide you.

You realize that this financial stewardship is about more than just money. It's about building a solid foundation for your blended family, creating a legacy of wisdom and generosity that will benefit your children for years. And just as the parable teaches, it's about faithfully managing what you've been entrusted with, multiplying those resources for the good of your family and others.

As you look toward the future, you feel a sense of hope and purpose. Yes, there will be challenges along the way, but you and your spouse are committed to facing them together. You're not just managing money – investing in your family's future, one wise decision at a time.

Critical Solutions for Stewarding Family Resources in Blended Families:

- Embrace generosity and contentment: Focus on being satisfied with what you have while finding ways to give to others. This mindset helps avoid the pitfalls of constant comparison and overspending.

- Implement wise planning and budgeting: Take the time to understand your financial situation thoroughly. Use tools like spreadsheets or budgeting apps to track expenses and income. Set clear financial goals as a family and create a plan to achieve them.

- Maintain open communication about money: Regular, honest discussions about finances are crucial in blended families. Openly and respectfully address different spending habits, financial obligations, and long-term goals.

- Address intricate monetary matters with expert assistance: Consult financial specialists or attorneys on non-traditional family arrangements, particularly for support payments, spousal maintenance, and inheritance planning.

- Teach children financial stewardship: Implement age-appropriate money lessons, model responsible financial behavior, and encourage charitable giving. This investment in your children's financial education will benefit them far into the future.

As you implement these solutions, remember that stewarding your family's resources is ongoing. It requires patience, flexibility, and continuous learning and adjustment. But with these principles as your guide, you're well-equipped to navigate blended family life's financial challenges and opportunities.

Your journey in financial stewardship continues. As you move forward, keep the lessons of the Parable of the Talents close to heart. Like faithful servants, you can multiply the resources entrusted to you – not just for your benefit but for the good of your entire blended family.

As you master the art of managing your earthly resources, remember that there's an even more significant investment to be made—in your spiritual lives. Our next chapter will focus on this balance between material and spiritual stewardship, exploring how to nurture your family's financial health and spiritual well-being.

Take a moment to appreciate the steps you've taken today. You've laid a strong foundation for your family's financial future. With continued effort and applying these principles, you're well on your way to creating a legacy of wise stewardship that will benefit your blended family for future generations.

As you close your planning session and look ahead to the rest of your day, you feel renewed in purpose and direction. You're not just managing money—investing in your family's future, nurturing relationships, and building a strong, unified, blended family. And that, you realize, is the greatest return on investment you could hope for.

CHAPTER TEN

Nurturing Spiritual Growth in Your Blended Family

"The family is, so to speak, the domestic church." - Pope John Paul II.

As you sit at your kitchen table, sipping your morning coffee, you can't help but smile at the chaos unfolding around you. Your stepson, Jake, is frantically searching for his math homework while your daughter, Emily, argues with her stepsister, Sophia, about whose turn it is to use the bathroom first. Your spouse rushes in, grabs a piece of toast, and gives you a quick kiss before heading out the door to work.

This is your blended family - beautiful, messy, and whole of life. But amidst the day-to-day hustle and bustle, you can't shake the feeling that something is missing. You've done your best to create a loving home, but there's a spiritual void you long to fill.

You remember growing up in a household where faith was central, where your parents made time for prayer and worship even on the busiest days. You want that for your blended family, too, but you need help figuring out where to start. How do you nurture spiritual growth when juggling different backgrounds, beliefs, and busy schedules?

Take a deep breath. You're not alone in this journey. Many blended families struggle to find their spiritual footing, but with patience, creativity, and grace, it's possible to create a home where faith flourishes and souls thrive.

Family Worship and Prayer

Let's start with Sarah and Tom, who faced similar challenges when they blended their families three years ago. Sarah brought two children from her previous marriage, while Tom had one. Both had grown up in Christian homes but had drifted away from regular church attendance in their adult years.

"We knew we wanted faith to be a part of our new family," Sarah explains, "but it initially felt awkward. The kids weren't used to praying together, and Tom and I weren't sure how to lead."

They decided to start small, with a simple prayer before dinner each night. At first, it felt forced and uncomfortable. The kids fidgeted, and there were more than a few eye rolls. But Sarah and Tom persevered.

"We kept it short and sweet," Tom says. It was a quick 'thank you' for our food and family. But over time, something shifted. The kids started volunteering to say the prayer. They began mentioning things they were grateful for or asking for help with challenges they were facing."

This small success encouraged Sarah and Tom to expand their family's spiritual practices. They established a daily devotional time and experimented with different approaches to find what worked best for their blended family.

Establishing daily devotional times

You might be wondering how to start this practice in your own home. Here are a few ideas that worked for Sarah and Tom:

1. Start with a consistent time and place. They chose to gather in the living room every evening after dinner.

2. Keep it brief, especially at first. They began by reading a short Bible passage or devotional story for 10 minutes.

3. Make it interactive. They encouraged questions and discussions, allowing even the youngest child to contribute.

4. Use age-appropriate materials. They found children's Bibles and devotionals that engaged their kids at different developmental stages.

5. Be flexible. Some nights, their devotional time became a deep discussion about faith and life. On other nights, with tired kids and busy schedules, they shared a brief prayer.

As you implement these practices, remember that consistency is critical. It may feel awkward or forced initially but don't give up. Your persistence will pay off as family worship becomes a natural and anticipated part of your day.

Praying for and with each family member

Sarah and Tom also discovered the power of praying for and with each family member individually. This practice helped bridge some initial awkwardness in their blended family and created deeper bonds.

"I started tucking in each of the kids at night, even the teenagers," Sarah shares. "I'd ask if there was anything they wanted me to pray about for them. At first, they were hesitant, but over time, they opened up. It became a special time for us to connect one-on-one."

Tom took a different approach. He left little notes in lunch boxes and backpacks, letting the kids know he prayed for their test or soccer game that afternoon. "It was my way of saying, 'I'm thinking about you and rooting for you,'" he explains. "And it opened up conversations about faith in a natural way."

You can adopt similar practices in your own family:

- Create a prayer board where family members can write prayer requests.

- Start a family prayer journal, taking turns writing entries.

- Use meal times to share challenges and victories, praying together for each person's needs.

- Send text messages or leave notes to let family members know you're praying for them.

Remember that the objective is to foster an environment where spiritual communication becomes a seamless, continuous aspect of household interactions rather than a structured practice limited to designated moments.

Adapting spiritual practices for different ages and backgrounds

One of Sarah and Tom's most significant challenges was adapting their spiritual practices to suit their blended family's different ages and backgrounds. Their children ranged from 8 to 16 years old, with varying levels of previous religious education.

"We had to get creative," Tom admits. Our youngest was excited about Bible stories and loved acting them out, but our teenager needed something more mature to engage with."

They found that a mix of activities worked best:

- For younger children: Bible story books, animated religious videos, and hands-on crafts related to Bible lessons.

- For pre-teens: Comic book-style Bibles, devotionals written for their age group, and discussion-based lessons.

- For teenagers: More in-depth Bible study, apologetics materials, and conversations about how faith relates to current events and personal challenges.

Sarah adds, "We also had to be sensitive to the fact that some of the kids had different religious experiences in their past. We clarified that questions were welcome and that it was okay to disagree or be unsure."

As you navigate this in your family, remember that flexibility and open communication are crucial. Be willing to try different approaches and ask your children for feedback. What works for one may not work for another, and that's okay.

Serving Together as a Family

As Sarah and Tom's family grew in their faith, they desired to put that faith into action. They wanted their children to understand that being a person of faith meant more than just attending church or reading the Bible - it meant living out those beliefs in tangible ways.

"We wanted to show our kids that faith isn't just something you do on Sundays," Sarah explains. "It's a way of life that involves serving others and making a difference in the world."

Finding volunteer opportunities

Their journey into family service started small. They signed up to serve meals at a local homeless shelter once a month. At first, some kids were reluctant, unsure of what to expect.

"I remember our first time at the shelter," Tom recalls. "Our oldest, Jason, was standoffish, barely making eye contact with the people we were serving. But by the night's end, he was deep in conversation with a veteran who had fallen on hard times. It was a transformative experience for him."

Over time, serving at the shelter became a family tradition everyone looked forward to. It opened up conversations about gratitude, compassion, and social justice that might not have happened otherwise.

You can start this practice in your own family by:

- Researching local volunteer opportunities that are appropriate for all ages.

- Allowing each family member to suggest causes they're passionate about.

- Starting with short-term or one-time commitments before making long-term commitments.

- Reflecting together after each service experience, discussing what you learned and how it relates to your faith.

Supporting missions and charities

Inspired by their experiences at the homeless shelter, Sarah and Tom's family began to look for other ways to make a difference. They decided to sponsor a child through an international charity, choosing a child close in age to their youngest.

"It was a way to connect our kids to the wider world," Sarah says. "We hung our sponsored child's picture on the fridge, and the kids took turns writing letters to her. It made global poverty real to them like statistics never could."

The family also started a tradition of choosing a different charity each holiday season to support. They would research organizations together, deciding where to donate a portion of their holiday budget as a family.

You might consider similar practices:

- Sponsor a child or project as a family, involving everyone in communication and support.

- Set aside a portion of allowances or family income for charitable giving, letting kids have a say in where it goes.

- Participate in charity walks, runs, or other fundraising events as a family team.

- Use holidays and birthdays as opportunities to give to others instead of some gifts.

Helping neighbors and community members

While supporting global causes was important to Sarah and Tom's family, they also wanted to make a difference in their immediate community. They began to look for ways to help their neighbors intentionally.

"We started small," Tom says. "We'd rake leaves for the elderly couple next door or shovel their driveway when it snowed. The kids grumbled initially, but soon they suggested ways we could help."

One summer, they decided to host a free car wash for their neighborhood. They set up in their driveway with signs offering "Free Car Washes - Just Because We Care." The event became an impromptu block party, with neighbors bringing refreshments and joining the fun.

"It was amazing to see how a simple act of kindness could unite the whole neighborhood," Sarah reflects. "It showed our kids that living out our faith can be fun and community-building."

Consider these ideas for serving in your community:

- Create a family "kindness calendar," planning one act of service each week.

- Participate in community clean-up days or beautification projects.

- Offer to babysit for single parents in your neighborhood or church.

- Host a free event for your community, like a car wash, bake sale, or game night.

As you engage in these service activities, remember to connect them back to your faith. Discuss how your actions reflect the teachings of your religion and how serving others expresses your beliefs.

Addressing Faith Differences

Despite their best efforts to create a unified family faith life, Sarah and Tom encountered challenges in addressing differences in beliefs and practices within their blended family.

"We hadn't realized how much our kids' previous experiences with religion would impact our new family dynamics," Sarah admits. "My ex-husband wasn't religious, so my kids had limited exposure to faith. On the other hand, Tom's son was raised in a very strict religious household and questioned much of what he'd been taught."

This situation isn't uncommon in blended families. You may find yourself navigating a mix of beliefs, doubts, and varying levels of religious education. The key is to create an environment of respect, open communication, and authentic faith exploration.

Respecting diverse beliefs within the family

Sarah and Tom made a conscious decision to respect the diverse beliefs within their family, even when those beliefs differed from their own. They established some ground rules:

1. No mocking or belittling others' beliefs.

2. Everyone has the right to ask questions and express doubts.

3. It's okay to say, "I don't know," or "I'm not sure."

4. We can disagree without being disagreeable.

"We wanted our home to be a safe place for spiritual exploration," Tom explains. "We didn't want to force our beliefs on the kids, but we did want to share why our faith was important to us."

This approach created an atmosphere where the children felt comfortable discussing their thoughts and questions about faith. Even when they disagreed, they learned to do so respectfully.

In your own family, consider:

- Having open discussions about different beliefs encourages each person to share their perspective.

- Acknowledging that doubt and questioning are standard parts of faith development.

- Modeling respect for other religions and worldviews, even if you disagree.

- This allows each family member agency in their spiritual journey while providing guidance and structure.

Encouraging questions and exploration

Sarah and Tom found that encouraging questions and exploration were crucial in addressing faith differences in their family. They started a weekly "Faith Q&A" session where family members could anonymously submit questions about religion, spirituality, or morality.

"Some of the questions were pretty challenging," Sarah recalls. They ranged from 'Why does God allow suffering?' to

'How do we know our religion is the right one?' We sometimes had answers, but we would research together and discuss honestly.

They also explored other faiths and denominations together. They visited different houses of worship, read books about various religions, and invited friends from different faith backgrounds to share their perspectives.

"We wanted our kids to understand why we believe what we believe," Tom says. "But we also wanted them to respect and understand other viewpoints. We believe that a faith that can't withstand questions or comparisons isn't firm."

To encourage questions and exploration in your family:

- Create a judgment-free zone for asking questions about faith.

- Use resources like books, documentaries, or online courses to explore different beliefs together.

- Attend interfaith events or visit various houses of worship as a family.

- Encourage critical thinking and personal reflection about spiritual matters.

Modeling authentic faith

The most potent tool Sarah and Tom found in addressing faith differences was modeling authentic faith in their own lives. They realized their actions spoke louder than words when influencing their children's spiritual development.

"We needed to demonstrate our beliefs through actions, not just words," Sarah explains. "This involved being transparent about our uncertainties and difficulties, acknowledging our errors, and illustrating how our spiritual convictions guided us through life's obstacles."

The couple allowed their children to witness them engaging in prayer, studying sacred writings, and grappling with complex spiritual issues. They openly shared how their faith influenced their reasoning and choices when confronted with decisions.

"One of the most impactful moments was when I lost my job," Tom shares. Instead of hiding our stress from the kids, we were open about our fears and trusting God to provide for us. It was a real-life lesson in faith that no sermon could have replicated."

To model authentic faith in your family:

- Be transparent about your spiritual journey, including

doubts and growth.

- Let your children see how your faith influences your daily decisions and actions.

- Admit when you don't have all the answers, and model how to seek wisdom and guidance.

- Share personal stories of how your faith has helped you overcome challenges or grow.

As we conclude this chapter, let's reflect on the transformative power of faith in blended families. While the journey may not always be smooth, nurturing spiritual growth can provide a strong foundation for family unity, purpose, and resilience.

Remember these kcy points as you cultivate faith in your blended family:

- Consistency is key. Start small with regular prayer or devotional times, and build from there.

- Serve together. Put your faith into action by finding ways to help others as a family.

- Honor varying perspectives. Establish an environment that welcomes inquiries, uncertainties, and a range of spiritual viewpoints.

- Model authentic faith. Let your actions and transparency speak louder than words.

- Exercise forbearance. Faith development is an ongoing process, not a fixed endpoint. Acknowledge and appreciate minor progress throughout the journey.

Your blended family is uniquely beautiful, with its challenges and blessings. As you nurture spiritual growth together, you're not just building a family - creating a domestic church where love, faith, and grace intersect in powerful ways. Embrace the journey, imperfections and all, and watch your family grow stronger in faith and unity with each passing day.

CONCLUSION

Embracing God's Vision for Your Blended Family

As you sit on the porch swing, gently rocking back and forth, you can't help but smile. The sound of laughter drifts through the open windows, a harmonious mix of voices that once seemed discordant but now blend perfectly. Your blended family has come a long way, and while the journey hasn't always been easy, you wouldn't change it for the world.

You think back to the day when this all began when you and your spouse stood at the altar, hearts full of hope and a little trepidation. You knew blending two families would be challenging, but you were determined to make it work. Years later, you can see how God has worked in your lives, guiding you through the storms and celebrating with you in the sunshine.

Let's take a walk down memory lane together, shall we? Remember those first few months? The awkward family dinners, the tension-filled holidays, the arguments over discipline and household rules? It felt like you were trying to piece together a puzzle with mismatched pieces. But you persevered, leaning on your faith and each other for support.

There was that memorable Christmas when your stepson refused to participate in your family's traditional gift exchange, insisting that it wasn't "his" family. The hurt in your biological children's eyes was almost unbearable. You and your spouse spent hours that night in prayer, asking for guidance and patience. Did you know this moment would become a turning point in your family's journey?

The following day, you gathered everyone in the living room. Instead of forcing the issue, you decided to create a new tradition. You pulled out a large poster board and some markers and asked each family member to write down one thing they loved about their old family traditions and one new tradition they'd like to start. It wasn't an instant fix, but it was a start. Your stepson hesitantly wrote down "Mom's cinnamon rolls" under things he missed and "family game night" under new traditions he'd like to try.

That simple activity opened the door to more communication. You started having weekly family meetings where everyone could voice their concerns and suggestions. You made a point of celebrating the significant achievements and the tiny victories. Remember how proud you were when your stepdaughter finally called your house "home" for the first time?

Of course, it could have been smoother sailing. There were

still arguments, misunderstandings, and moments of frustration. But you learned to approach each challenge with grace, patience, and much prayer. You discovered that blending a family isn't about erasing the past or forcing instant bonds but about creating a new story that honors where you've all come from while embracing where you're going.

One of the biggest lessons you learned was the importance of unity between you and your spouse. You realized you needed to present a united front for your blended family to thrive. This meant having difficult conversations behind closed doors, supporting each other's decisions before the kids, and always putting your marriage first.

Remember that family vacation to the beach? It was the first time you all traveled together, and tensions were high. Your kids were upset about sharing a room with their step-siblings, and your stepchildren were homesick for their other parent. You and your spouse felt like walking on eggshells, trying to keep everyone happy.

But then, something beautiful happened. A storm rolled in, confining everyone to the beach house. Instead of letting the close quarters breed more conflict, you saw an opportunity. You dug out some board games from the closet, made hot chocolate, and declared a family game tournament. As the rain pattered against the windows and the wind howled outside, something shifted inside. Laughter replaced complaints, teamwork overshadowed individual grievances, and by the time the storm cleared, your family had weathered more than just the elements.

That vacation became a turning point. You all returned home with inside jokes, shared experiences, and a new appreciation for each other. It wasn't perfect – blended families rarely are – but it was progress. You learned that sometimes, the storms in life aren't meant to break us but to bring us closer together.

As your family grew and changed, you discovered the power of flexibility. You learned to adjust your expectations and celebrate your blended family's unique dynamics rather than trying to force it into a traditional mold. You embraced the idea that love multiplies; it doesn't divide. There was enough love to go around, even if it looked different than you initially imagined.

One of the most challenging aspects was dealing with the children's other biological parent. There were times when conflicting schedules, different parenting styles, and old hurts threatened to derail the progress you'd made. But you chose to take the high road, always speaking respectfully about the other parent in front of the children and finding ways to co-parent effectively despite the challenges.

You remember the day your stepdaughter came home in tears because she felt torn between her two families. Instead of becoming defensive or hurt, you listened. You assured her it was okay to love both families and that she didn't have to choose. You even contacted her mother, suggesting you attend her next school play together to show unified support. It wasn't easy, but the smile on your stepdaughter's face when she saw all her parents in the audience together was worth every ounce of effort.

Through it all, you kept God at the center of your family. You prayed, studied Scripture, and sought guidance from your church community. You learned to see each family member through God's eyes – as precious, unique, and worthy of love. This perspective shift made all the difference in how you approached conflicts and celebrated joys.

Now, as you sit on that porch swing, you can see the fruits of your labor. Your once-fractured family has become a testament to God's grace and the power of perseverance. The kids who once bickered constantly now defend each other fiercely. The stepchildren who once felt like outsiders now bring their friends over, proudly introducing you as their parent. Your spouse, once overwhelmed by the challenges of blending families, now beams with pride at what you've built together.

But you know the work isn't over. Blended families, like all families, require constant nurturing and attention. As you look towards the future, you feel a sense of excitement rather than dread. You've learned that each challenge is an opportunity for growth, each conflict a chance to deepen understanding, and each day a gift to be cherished.

So, dear reader, remember that God has a beautiful vision for your family as you navigate your blended family journey. It may not look like what you initially imagined, but it's filled with more love, growth, and blessings than you could have dreamed. Embrace this vision, lean into the challenges, and watch God work miracles in your midst.

Here are some key takeaways to help you implement God's vision for your blended family:

- Prioritize unity with your spouse: Present a united front to the children, support each other's decisions, and nurture your marriage as the foundation of your blended family.

- Create new traditions while honoring the old: Find ways to blend traditions with new ones, creating a unique family culture that respects everyone's history.

- Keep God at the center: Pray together, study Scripture as a family, and view each family member through God's eyes.

- Embrace flexibility: Be willing to adjust your expectations and celebrate the unique dynamics of your blended family.

- Practice patience and perseverance: Building a strong blended family takes time. Celebrate small victories and learn from challenges.

As you close this chapter of our book, please take a moment to envision your blended family five years from now. See the bonds that have strengthened, the love that has deepened, and the faith that has grown. This vision isn't just a dream – it's God's plan for your family. With His guidance and your commitment, you can create a thriving, Christ-centered blended family that becomes a beacon of hope and love to others.

Your journey as a blended family is unique and filled with challenges and blessings. There will be days when you feel like you're taking two steps forward and one step back. In those moments, remember the stories we've shared, the principles we've discussed, and most importantly, the unwavering love of God that brought your family together.

Think back to the family in our story. They turned a stormy beach vacation into a bonding experience, created new traditions while honoring the old, and navigated co-parenting challenges gracefully. These aren't just lovely stories; they're roadmaps for your journey. You can turn your challenges into opportunities and your conflicts into connections.

Remember, blending a family is not about creating a perfect replica of a traditional family unit. It's about weaving together the unique threads of each family member's experiences, personalities, and love into a beautiful, one-of-a-kind tapestry. Your family's story is still being written, and with God's help, it will be an epic tale of love, redemption, and joy.

As you move forward, please intentionally implement the strategies we've discussed. Start with small steps – perhaps begin with a family meeting where everyone can share their thoughts and feelings openly. Or maybe initiate a new family tradition incorporating original family elements. Keep in mind that significant shifts rarely occur instantly. However, modest, regular efforts can result in substantial alterations as time progresses.

Don't be discouraged if you face setbacks. Every family, blended or not, encounters obstacles. The key is how you respond to these challenges. See them as opportunities to grow closer as a family, to lean more heavily on God, and to demonstrate the unconditional love that Christ modeled for us.

Celebrate your progress, no matter how small it may seem. Did your stepchild confide in you for the first time? Celebrate it. Did you successfully navigate a potentially contentious holiday without significant conflicts? That's worth acknowledging. Did your children from different original families choose to sit together at school lunch? Rejoice in that victory. These moments are the building blocks of your blended family's success story.

Remember to care for yourself and your marriage amidst the challenges of blending families. It's easy to get so caught up in meeting everyone else's needs that you neglect your own. Make time for self-care, date nights with your spouse, and quiet moments of prayer and reflection. A strong, healthy you and a strong marriage are crucial foundations for a thriving blended family.

As we conclude this journey together, I want to leave you with a vision of hope. Close your eyes and picture your family gathered around the dinner table. Everyone gets laughter, animated conversation, and inside jokes. Your spouse catches your eye across the table, and you share a smile, both thinking about how far you've come. Your children and stepchildren are engaged in friendly banter, and their sibling bonds are evident in their interactions. There's a sense of belonging, of unity, of love that permeates the air.

This isn't just a pleasant daydream—this is God's vision for your blended family. It's a vision of healing, restored relationships, and love that transcends biological connections. It's a vision of a family that reflects God's unconditional love and grace to a world that desperately needs it.

You have the power to make this vision a reality. It won't always be easy, but remember – you're not alone in this journey. You have the support of your spouse, the love of your children, the guidance of God, and now, the knowledge and strategies we've explored together in this book.

So, what's your next step? It may be initiating that family meeting we talked about. Maybe it's having a heart-to-heart with your spouse about better supporting each other. It could be reaching out to a stepchild you've struggled to connect with. Whatever it is, I encourage you to take that step today. Don't wait for the perfect moment – create it.

Your blended family is a good decision and a second-best option. It's a beautiful, complex, divinely orchestrated unit with the potential to showcase God's love uniquely and powerfully. Embrace this truth. Allow it to shape your behavior, influence your choices, and sustain your determination during challenging periods.

As you close this book and step back into your daily life, carry the stories, strategies, and encouragement we've shared. Remember that you're writing a love story – not just between you and your spouse, but a grand narrative of God's redemptive love played out in the lives of your blended family. Every day is a new page in this story. Fill it with grace, patience, understanding, and love.

Your blended family journey is just beginning. Challenges will be ahead, but there will also be joy, growth, and love beyond measure. Trust in God's plan, lean on His strength, and watch as He transforms your blended family into a masterpiece of His grace.

Go forth with confidence, dear reader. Your blended family is blessed and loved and has a bright future ahead. Embrace God's vision for your family and let His love guide you every step of the way. The best is yet to come!

About the Author

Rev. Dr. Sean Alexander, Ph.D., is a multifaceted professional dedicated to helping others experience the love of God in their lives. As the President of the International Corps of

Chaplains, he's significantly impacting people's lives. His roles extend into being the Presiding Archbishop of the Archdiocese of the Sacred Heart, a Christian Clinical Therapist, and a Life Coach, all of which showcase his diverse expertise.

Based in Central Florida, Dr. Alexander specializes in Christian Marriage and Family Therapy, addressing issues like depression and anxiety with a holistic approach. Thanks to his online sessions, his unique blend of biblical wisdom and modern therapeutic techniques is transforming lives across Florida and beyond. With his warm personality and deep faith, Dr. Alexander isn't just a therapist—he's a beacon of hope for those seeking guidance and healing.

DrSeanAlexander.org

Acknowledgments

Rev. Dr. Sean Alexander extends his heartfelt gratitude to the following:

First and foremost, thank God for His unwavering guidance and the calling to serve others.

His ministry family's endless love, support, and patience throughout his journey.

To the dedicated team at Chaplains International Inc., whose unwavering commitment to global outreach inspires and makes the professional community feel appreciated and recognized.

He thanks his mentors at the National Board of Christian Clinical Therapists and the American Association of Christian Counseling for their wisdom and encouragement.

To the faculty at Coachville's Graduate School of Coaching for equipping him with invaluable skills.

To his colleagues in therapy and ministry for their collaborative spirit and shared passion for healing.

To his clients, past and present, for their trust and for allowing him to be part of their growth journeys.

To the many communities he serves in for embracing his practice and mission.

Finally, your belief in this work has made all the difference to all those who have supported his vision of integrating faith, psychology, and holistic healing.